Biodiversity

Other Books in the Current Controversies Series

Biodiversity

Debra A. Miller, Book Editor

GREENHAVEN PRESS
A part of Gale, Cengage Learning

Detroit • New York • San Francisco • New Haven, Conn • Waterville, Maine • London

Elizabeth Des Chenes, *Director, Publishing Solutions*

© 2013 Greenhaven Press, a part of Gale, Cengage Learning

Gale and Greenhaven Press are registered trademarks used herein under license.

For more information, contact:
Greenhaven Press
27500 Drake Rd.
Farmington Hills, MI 48331-3535
Or you can visit our Internet site at gale.cengage.com

Articles in Greenhaven Press anthologies are often edited for length to meet page requirements. In addition, original titles of these works are changed to clearly present the main thesis and to explicitly indicate the author's opinion. Every effort is made to ensure that Greenhaven Press accurately reflects the original intent of the authors. Every effort has been made to trace the owners of copyrighted material.

Cover image photoinnovation/Shutterstock.com.

LIBRARY OF CONGRESS CATALOGING-IN-PUBLICATION DATA

Biodiversity / Debra A. Miller, book editor.
    p. cm. -- (Current controversies)
    Summary: "Biodiversity: This series covers today's most current national and international issues and the most important opinions of the past and present. The purpose of the series is to introduce readers to all sides of contemporary controversies"-- Provided by publisher.
    Includes bibliographical references and index.
    ISBN 978-0-7377-6221-1 (hardback) -- ISBN 978-0-7377-6222-8 (paperback)
    1. Biodiversity--Juvenile literature. I. Miller, Debra A.
    QH541.15.B56B5576 2012
    333.95--dc23
                                                              2012022094

Printed in the United States of America
1 2 3 4 5 6 7 16 15 14 13 12

Contents

Chapter 2: Which Plant and Animal Species Are Threatened with Extinction?

Chapter 4: How Can Earth's Biodiversity Be Protected?

Foreword

By definition, controversies are "discussions of questions in which opposing opinions clash" (*Webster's Twentieth Century Dictionary Unabridged*). Few would deny that controversies are a pervasive part of the human condition and exist on virtually every level of human enterprise. Controversies transpire between individuals and among groups, within nations and between nations. Controversies supply the grist necessary for progress by providing challenges and challengers to the status quo. They also create atmospheres where strife and warfare can flourish. A world without controversies would be a peaceful world; but it also would be, by and large, static and prosaic.

The Series' Purpose

The purpose of the Current Controversies series is to explore many of the social, political, and economic controversies dominating the national and international scenes today. Titles selected for inclusion in the series are highly focused and specific. For example, from the larger category of criminal justice, Current Controversies deals with specific topics such as police brutality, gun control, white collar crime, and others. The debates in Current Controversies also are presented in a useful, timeless fashion. Articles and book excerpts included in each title are selected if they contribute valuable, long-range ideas to the overall debate. And wherever possible, current information is enhanced with historical documents and other relevant materials. Thus, while individual titles are current in focus, every effort is made to ensure that they will not become quickly outdated. Books in the Current Controversies series will remain important resources for librarians, teachers, and students for many years.

In addition to keeping the titles focused and specific, great care is taken in the editorial format of each book in the series. Book introductions and chapter prefaces are offered to provide background material for readers. Chapters are organized around several key questions that are answered with diverse opinions representing all points on the political spectrum. Materials in each chapter include opinions in which authors clearly disagree as well as alternative opinions in which authors may agree on a broader issue but disagree on the possible solutions. In this way, the content of each volume in Current Controversies mirrors the mosaic of opinions encountered in society. Readers will quickly realize that there are many viable answers to these complex issues. By questioning each author's conclusions, students and casual readers can begin to develop the critical thinking skills so important to evaluating opinionated material.

Current Controversies is also ideal for controlled research. Each anthology in the series is composed of primary sources taken from a wide gamut of informational categories including periodicals, newspapers, books, US and foreign government documents, and the publications of private and public organizations. Readers will find factual support for reports, debates, and research papers covering all areas of important issues. In addition, an annotated table of contents, an index, a book and periodical bibliography, and a list of organizations to contact are included in each book to expedite further research.

Perhaps more than ever before in history, people are confronted with diverse and contradictory information. During the Persian Gulf War, for example, the public was not only treated to minute-to-minute coverage of the war, it was also inundated with critiques of the coverage and countless analyses of the factors motivating US involvement. Being able to sort through the plethora of opinions accompanying today's major issues, and to draw one's own conclusions, can be a complicated and frustrating struggle. It is the editors' hope that Current Controversies will help readers with this struggle.

Introduction

> "[Biodiversity] is not only important to a
> healthy global environment and climate;
> it also is vital to human life itself—the
> human food supply, human health, and
> the worldwide economy."

Scientific experts agree that humans are damaging Earth's *biodiversity*, a term that comprises the total variety of plant and animal forms on the planet. More specifically, the Convention on Biological Diversity (CBD), an international environmental treaty, defines biodiversity as "the variability among living organisms from all sources including, inter alia, terrestrial, marine and other aquatic ecosystems and the ecological complexes of which they are part; this includes diversity within species, between species and of ecosystems."[1] This intricate web of life is not only important to a healthy global environment and climate; it also is vital to human life itself—the human food supply, human health, and the worldwide economy.

The starting point for many people in explaining the importance of biodiversity is that it has inherent value; that is, each creature and life form on Earth has a fundamental right to exist. Many cultures and religions support the idea that nature is holy and that humans have a duty to protect it. The biblical story of Noah, for example, tells how Noah saved a pair of every creature on Earth from the flood. Although the Bible passages giving humans dominion have been used by some to justify human exploitation of nature, many religious scholars argue that this is a misinterpretation. The correct interpretation, they maintain, is that humans are stewards of the environment and have a responsibility to protect Earth's biodiversity.

Even if humans have no moral or ethical duty to prevent biodiversity loss, however, experts argue there are many other reasons to do so. The planet has evolved over billions of years, slowly creating a delicately balanced environmental system that employs natural processes to regulate global weather, purify the air, and absorb wastes, providing a perfect home for diverse forms of life, including humans. Tiny soil organisms, for example, break down wastes to make nutrients such as nitrogen available to plants. Insects, birds, and other creatures help in plant pollination and reproduction. Plants absorb carbon dioxide and release oxygen into the atmosphere, which is necessary for marine life and mammals. Ecosystems such as coastal wetlands help to filter contaminants and mitigate or prevent flooding, erosion, and other natural disasters. In this complex biosphere system, each life form is connected to every other, and the loss of life forms eventually affects all ecosystems. Studies have shown, for example, that the loss of one key animal species can affect an ecosystem's entire food chain, including the types of plants that flourish or die in the region. Nature's great diversity is also a buffer against global warming, giving the environment resilience in the face of climate changes and weather events that threaten species' survival.

Biodiversity also is essential to human survival in many other ways. Perhaps most importantly, it is the foundation of modern agriculture and human food security. All of the world's main food crops and animals—such as wheat, corn, soybeans, and livestock—are derived from what were once wild plants and animals and are dependent on wild genetic sources for their continued survival and improvement. Even biotech industries that are devising new genetic strains of genetically engineered crops use wild plants as a source of genetic material. In addition, wild fish populations in oceans, rivers, and lakes are the main source of protein for many people around the world.

Biodiversity is also important to human health. The medical profession relies on many drugs that were derived from chemical substances found in wild plants and animals. These include common over-the-counter drugs such as aspirin as well as many prescription drugs used around the world. More traditional, indigenous medicine systems, such as Chinese herbal medicine, depend even more directly on wild plants and their cultivated cousins. Yet only a tiny number of known plant species have been screened for their medicinal qualities, and new drugs are being discovered and developed all the time. For example, certain drugs used to treat cancer have been developed from natural plant sources.

Biodiversity is necessary, too, to support jobs and the global economy. In addition to the economic value created by agriculture, fishing, medicines, and the trade of wild plants and animals, biodiversity supplies humans with a wealth of other substances that are turned into clothes, construction materials, and many other highly valued products. In fact, some studies have found that forests, reefs, and oceans provide up to 89 percent of the income of rural and poor households in many developing countries. Biodiversity provides humans with other valuable gifts as well, such as a wide variety of recreational activities and income from tourism. A recent estimate put the total economic value to businesses of a functioning biosphere at somewhere around $33 trillion per year.

Yet scientists warn that human activities—everything from agriculture and exploitation of natural resources to industrial pollution, urban sprawl, and population growth—are taking a heavy toll on biodiversity, affecting the global climate and threatening or wiping out both plant and animal species at an unprecedented rate. Global warming is perhaps the biggest threat to biodiversity. The burning of fossil fuels for transportation, industry, electricity production, and home heating releases carbon dioxide and other greenhouse gases into the atmosphere, causing global climate changes. The resulting disruptions in climate, in turn, force many animals to migrate and plants to change, but in many cases conditions change too fast to allow species the time to adapt, threatening many species with habitat loss and possible extinction. Deforestation and other habitat destruction, introduction of invasive species, overfishing, and overhunting put great pressure on many species and cause what many experts say is an unprecedented rate of species extinction. At the present rate, some scientists have predicted, half of Earth's plant and animal species might be gone by the end of the twenty-first century.

There are some bright spots, however. One hundred and sixty-eight countries have signed the Convention on Biological Diversity and over the past decade have made progress in creating protected habitat areas, slowing rainforest destruction, and taking other actions to reduce biodiversity loss. Some studies suggest that species loss may take longer than once believed, giving people more time to address the problem. Still, many experts say that much more needs to be done immediately to prevent irreversible damage to the planet. The authors of the viewpoints in *Current Controversies: Biodiversity* examine the many issues surrounding this environmental topic, including the seriousness of biodiversity loss, the growing rate of extinction, the dangers in modern food methods, and possible future steps to be taken to protect biodiversity.

Notes

1. Convention on Biological Diversity, Article 2, accessed May 21, 2012. www.cbd.int/convention/articles/?a=cbd-02.doc.

CHAPTER 1

Is Biodiversity Loss a Serious Problem?

Chapter Preface

China has long been one of the most populated countries on the planet, but today it is also one of the fastest developing nations. During the first decade of the twenty-first century, China's economy exploded, growing at a rate of about 10 percent a year. In 2011, China overtook Japan as the world's second biggest economy. This remarkable economic growth, however, is happening at the expense of China's once rich environment, which is said to contain as much as 10 percent of the world's biodiversity. Although many Chinese still live very simply compared to Americans, Chinese consumption rates are steadily increasing, and providing food, jobs, housing, and consumer goods to more than 1.3 billion people is posing unprecedented threats to the biodiversity of China as well as the rest of the world.

By far the biggest biodiversity threat in China comes from habitat destruction. The nation has undertaken huge engineering endeavors to build hydroelectric plants that change the flow of its rivers, convert wetlands into farmlands, and use flood plains for construction and infrastructure projects. At the same time, deforestation, overgrazing, unsustainable agricultural practices (including the liberal use of chemical fertilizers), and dwindling water sources are eroding the soil, turning large tracts of the country into desert, and causing sandstorms that blow around the world. Some estimates say up to 30 percent of China's land has been lost to desertification, and some villages in central China have been abandoned because people can no longer farm or make a living in them.

Meanwhile, China's development is creating massive air and water pollution. China's power plants—more than 75 percent of which are still dependent on coal—crank out greenhouse gases and pollutants even as the demand for automobiles is rapidly increasing, adding to the pollution levels.

According to a 2007 World Bank report, twenty of the world's thirty most polluted cities are in China. Yet because of the great demand for energy, China is still building new coal-powered power stations, despite the pollution danger. As a result of this air pollution, respiratory and heart diseases are the leading cause of death in China. Water pollution is just as bad as air pollution. Untreated wastes from manufacturing plants and urban areas have historically been dumped into China's rivers, and the creation of new economic zones along some of the biggest rivers, such as the Yangtze, are only adding to the damage. Water quality in many Chinese rivers is no longer fit for human consumption.

Economic projects, overuse of resources, pollution, and poor environmental protections have seriously damaged ecosystems and destroyed habitat for many of China's animal and plant species. Even China's famous giant pandas are threatened because many of their forest homes have been consumed by agricultural uses and timber and fuel production. Today, the giant panda's original forest habitat has been sharply reduced. In addition, the Chinese continue to hunt and kill endangered wildlife, such as tigers that live in the country's temperate rainforests, to produce food and traditional Chinese medicines. In fact, more than one-fourth of all the species listed as critically endangered by the Convention on International Trade in Endangered Species (CITES)—an international treaty that seeks to protect endangered species from exploitation—are found in China. Species loss in China, some experts say, is 50–100 percent higher than the global average.

The Chinese government has begun to wake up to the nation's biodiversity crisis. Academics and nongovernmental organizations are also working on the problem. Perhaps the biggest government effort is a campaign launched in 2007—called the National Strategy for Plant Conservation—to try to slow and reverse biodiversity losses. This campaign largely follows the framework set forth in the Global Strategy for Plant

Conservation, a plan agreed to by over one hundred countries that have signed the Convention on Biological Diversity, the main international treaty directed at reducing biodiversity loss. The goals of the Chinese campaign include, for example: plans to convert millions of acres of farmland back to forests; a complete halt to logging in many of the nation's forests; a ban on all polluting development projects near key biodiversity areas; increased enforcement against illegal logging and farming; and funding for ecological research and management. China also hopes to encourage more sustainable agriculture practices nationwide and plans to conserve genes of native plants in a network of one hundred and sixty botanic gardens.

Although China is perhaps an extreme example, the loss of biodiversity is also an issue for most countries around the world. The authors of viewpoints in this chapter debate just how serious a problem biodiversity loss is and highlight some reasons for hope that this problem can be solved.

Global Biodiversity Losses Are Approaching Tipping Points of No Return

Secretariat of the Convention on Biological Diversity

The Convention on Biological Diversity (CBD) is one of the three Rio Conventions, or agreements, emerging from the UN Conference on Environment and Development, also known as the Earth Summit, held in Rio de Janeiro in 1992. It seeks the conservation of biological diversity and the sustainable and fair use of the natural world. The Secretariat of CBD was established to support the goals of the Convention.

The target agreed by the world's Governments in 2002, "to achieve by 2010 a significant reduction of the current rate of biodiversity loss at the global, regional and national level as a contribution to poverty alleviation and to the benefit of all life on Earth", has not been met.

Continuing Decline in Biodiversity

There are multiple indications of continuing decline in biodiversity in all three of its main components—genes, species and ecosystems—including:

- Species which have been assessed for extinction risk are on average moving closer to extinction. Amphibians face the greatest risk and coral species are deteriorating most rapidly in status. Nearly a quarter of plant species are estimated to be threatened with extinction.

- The abundance of vertebrate species, based on assessed populations, fell by nearly a third on average between

1970 and 2006, and continues to fall globally, with especially severe declines in the tropics and among freshwater species.

- Natural habitats in most parts of the world continue to decline in extent and integrity, although there has been significant progress in slowing the rate of loss for tropical forests and mangroves, in some regions. Freshwater wetlands, sea ice habitats, salt marshes, coral reefs, seagrass beds and shellfish reefs are all showing serious declines.

- Extensive fragmentation and degradation of forests, rivers and other ecosystems have also led to loss of biodiversity and ecosystem services.

- Crop and livestock genetic diversity continues to decline in agricultural systems.

- The five principal pressures directly driving biodiversity loss (habitat change, overexploitation, pollution, invasive alien species and climate change) are either constant or increasing in intensity.

- The ecological footprint of humanity exceeds the biological capacity of the Earth by a wider margin than at the time the 2010 target was agreed.

Insufficient Action to Support Biodiversity

The loss of biodiversity is an issue of profound concern for its own sake. Biodiversity also underpins the functioning of ecosystems which provide a wide range of services to human societies. Its continued loss, therefore, has major implications for current and future human well-being. The provision of food, fibre, medicines and fresh water, pollination of crops, filtration of pollutants, and protection from natural disasters are among those ecosystem services potentially threatened by declines and changes in biodiversity. Cultural services such as spiritual and religious values, opportunities for knowledge and education, as well as recreational and aesthetic values, are also declining.

The existence of the 2010 biodiversity target has helped to stimulate important action to safeguard biodiversity, such as creating more protected areas (both on land and in coastal waters), the conservation of particular species, and initiatives to tackle some of the direct causes of ecosystem damage, such as pollution and alien species invasions. Some 170 countries now have national biodiversity strategies and action plans. At the international level, financial resources have been mobilized and progress has been made in developing mechanisms for research, monitoring and scientific assessment of biodiversity.

Most future scenarios project continuing high levels of extinctions and loss of habitats throughout this century.

Many actions in support of biodiversity have had significant and measurable results in particular areas and amongst targeted species and ecosystems. This suggests that with adequate resources and political will, the tools exist for loss of biodiversity to be reduced at wider scales. For example, recent government policies to curb deforestation have been followed by declining rates of forest loss in some tropical countries. Measures to control alien invasive species have helped a number of species to move to a lower extinction risk category. It has been estimated that at least 31 bird species (out of 9,800) would have become extinct in the past century, in the absence of conservation measures.

However, action to implement the Convention on Biological Diversity has not been taken on a sufficient scale to address the pressures on biodiversity in most places. There has been insufficient integration of biodiversity issues into broader policies, strategies and programmes, and the underlying drivers of biodiversity loss have not been addressed significantly.

Actions to promote the conservation and sustainable use of biodiversity receive a tiny fraction of funding compared to activities aimed at promoting infrastructure and industrial developments. Moreover, biodiversity considerations are often ignored when such developments are designed, and opportunities to plan in ways that minimize unnecessary negative impacts on biodiversity are missed. Actions to address the underlying drivers of biodiversity loss, including demographic, economic, technological, socio-political and cultural pressures, in meaningful ways, have also been limited.

The Future

Most future scenarios project continuing high levels of extinctions and loss of habitats throughout this century, with associated decline of some ecosystem services important to human well-being.

For example:

- Tropical forests would continue to be cleared in favour of crops and pastures, and potentially for biofuel production.

- Climate change, the introduction of invasive alien species, pollution and dam construction would put further pressure on freshwater biodiversity and the services it underpins.

- Overfishing would continue to damage marine ecosystems and cause the collapse of fish populations, leading to the failure of fisheries.

Changes in the abundance and distribution of species may have serious consequences for human societies. The geographical distribution of species and vegetation types is projected to shift radically due to climate change, with ranges moving from hundreds to thousands of kilometres towards the poles by the end of the 21st century. Migration of marine species to cooler waters could make tropical oceans less diverse, while both boreal and temperate forests face widespread dieback at the southern end of their existing ranges, with impacts on fisheries, wood harvests, recreation opportunities and other services.

There is a high risk of dramatic biodiversity loss and accompanying degradation of a broad range of ecosystem services if ecosystems are pushed beyond certain thresholds or tipping points. The poor would face the earliest and most severe impacts of such changes, but ultimately all societies and communities would suffer.

Examples include:

- The Amazon forest, due to the interaction of deforestation, fire and climate change, could undergo a widespread dieback, with parts of the forest moving into a self-perpetuating cycle of more frequent fires and intense droughts leading to a shift to savanna-like vegetation. While there are large uncertainties associated with these scenarios, it is known that such dieback becomes much more likely to occur if deforestation exceeds 20–30% (it is currently above 17% in the Brazilian Amazon). It would lead to regional rainfall reductions, compromising agricultural production. There would also be global impacts through increased carbon emissions, and massive loss of biodiversity.

- The build-up of phosphates and nitrates from agricultural fertilizers and sewage effluent can shift freshwater lakes and other inland water ecosystems into a long-term, algae-dominated (eutrophic) state. This could lead to declining fish availability with implications for food security in many developing countries. There will also be loss of recreation opportunities and tourism income, and in some cases health risks for people and livestock from toxic algal blooms. Similar, nitrogen-induced eutrophication phenomena in coastal environments lead to more oxygen-starved dead zones, with major economic losses resulting from reduced productivity of fisheries and decreased tourism revenues.

- The combined impacts of ocean acidification, warmer sea temperatures and other human-induced stresses make tropical coral reef ecosystems vulnerable to collapse. More acidic water—brought about by higher carbon dioxide concentrations in the atmosphere—decreases the availability of the carbonate ions required to build coral skeletons. Together with the bleaching impact of warmer water, elevated nutrient levels from pollution, overfishing, sediment deposition arising from inland deforestation, and other pressures, reefs worldwide increasingly become algae-dominated with catastrophic loss of biodiversity and ecosystem functioning, threatening the livelihoods and food security of hundreds of millions of people.

The linked challenges of biodiversity loss and climate change must be addressed by policymakers . . . if the most severe impacts of each are to be avoided.

The Need for Better Protection of Biodiversity

There are greater opportunities than previously recognized to address the biodiversity crisis while contributing to other social objectives. For example, analyses conducted for this Outlook identified scenarios in which climate change is mitigated while maintaining and even expanding the current extent of forests and other natural ecosystems (avoiding additional habitat loss from the widespread deployment of biofuels). Other opportunities include "rewilding" abandoned farmland in some regions, and the restoration of river basins and other wetland ecosystems to enhance water supply, flood control and the removal of pollutants.

Well-targeted policies focusing on critical areas, species and ecosystem services are essential to avoid the most dangerous impacts on people and societies. Preventing further human-induced biodiversity loss for the near-term future will be extremely challenging, but biodiversity loss may be halted and in some aspects reversed in the longer term, if urgent, concerted and effective action is initiated now in support of an agreed long-term vision. Such action to conserve biodiversity and use its components sustainably will reap rich rewards—through better health, greater food security, less poverty and a greater capacity to cope with, and adapt to, environmental change.

Placing greater priority on biodiversity is central to the success of development and poverty-alleviation measures. It is clear that continuing with "business as usual" will jeopardize the future of all human societies, and none more so than the poorest who depend directly on biodiversity for a particularly high proportion of their basic needs. The loss of biodiversity is frequently linked to the loss of cultural diversity, and has an especially high negative impact on indigenous communities.

The linked challenges of biodiversity loss and climate change must be addressed by policymakers with equal priority and in close co-ordination, if the most severe impacts of each are to be avoided. Reducing the further loss of carbon-storing ecosystems such as tropical forests, salt marshes and peatlands will be a crucial step in limiting the build-up of greenhouse gases in the atmosphere. At the same time, reducing other pressures on ecosystems can increase their resilience, make them less vulnerable to those impacts of climate change which are already unavoidable, and allow them to continue to provide services to support people's livelihoods and help them adapt to climate change.

Better protection of biodiversity should be seen as a prudent and cost-effective investment in risk-avoidance for the global community. The consequences of abrupt ecosystem changes on a large scale affect human security to such an extent, that it is rational to minimize the risk of triggering them—even if we are not clear about the precise probability that they will occur. Ecosystem degradation, and the consequent loss of ecosystem services, has been identified as one of the main sources of disaster risk. Investment in resilient and diverse ecosystems, able to withstand the multiple pressures they are subjected to, may be the best-value insurance policy yet devised.

Scientific uncertainty surrounding the precise connections between biodiversity and human well-being, and the functioning of ecosystems, should not be used as an excuse for inaction. No one can predict with accuracy how close we are to ecosystem tipping points, and how much additional pressure might bring them about. What is known from past examples, however, is that once an ecosystem shifts to another state, it can be difficult or impossible to return it to the former conditions on which economies and patterns of settlement have been built for generations.

Urgent action is needed to reduce the direct drivers of biodiversity loss.

Addressing the Real Causes of Biodiversity Loss

Effective action to address biodiversity loss depends on addressing the underlying causes or indirect drivers of that decline.

This will mean:

- Much greater efficiency in the use of land, energy, fresh water and materials to meet growing demand.

- Use of market incentives, and avoidance of perverse subsidies, to minimize unsustainable resource use and wasteful consumption.

- Strategic planning in the use of land, inland waters and marine resources to reconcile development with conservation of biodiversity and the maintenance of multiple ecosystem services. While some actions may entail moderate costs or tradeoffs, the gains for biodiversity can be large in comparison.

- Ensuring that the benefits arising from use of and access to genetic resources and associated traditional knowledge, for example through the development of drugs and cosmetics, are equitably shared with the countries and cultures from which they are obtained.

- Communication, education and awareness-raising to ensure that as far as possible, everyone understands the value of biodiversity and what steps they can take to protect it, including through changes in personal consumption and behaviour.

The real benefits of biodiversity, and the costs of its loss, need to be reflected within economic systems and markets. Perverse subsidies and the lack of economic value attached to the huge benefits provided by ecosystems have contributed to the loss of biodiversity. Through regulation and other measures, markets can and must be harnessed to create incentives to safeguard and strengthen, rather than to deplete, our natural infrastructure. The re-structuring of economies and financial systems following the global recession provides an opportunity for such changes to be made. Early action will be both more effective and less costly than inaction or delayed action.

Urgent action is needed to reduce the direct drivers of biodiversity loss. The application of best practices in agriculture, sustainable forest management and sustainable fisheries should become standard practice, and approaches aimed at optimizing multiple ecosystem services instead of maximizing a single one should be promoted. In many cases, multiple drivers are combining to cause biodiversity loss and degradation of ecosystems. Sometimes, it may be more effective to concentrate urgent action on reducing those drivers most responsive to policy changes. This will reduce the pressures on biodiversity and protect its value for human societies in the short to medium-term, while the more intractable drivers are addressed over a longer time-scale. For example the resilience of coral reefs—and their ability to withstand and adapt to coral bleaching and ocean acidification—can be enhanced by reducing overfishing, land-based pollution and physical damage.

Direct action to conserve biodiversity must be continued, targeting vulnerable as well as culturally-valued species and ecosystems, combined with steps to safeguard key ecosystem services, particularly those of importance to the poor. Activities could focus on the conservation of species threatened with extinction, those harvested for commercial purposes, or species of cultural significance. They should also ensure the protection of functional ecological groups—that is, groups of species that collectively perform particular, essential roles within ecosystems, such as pollination, control of herbivore numbers by top predators, cycling of nutrients and soil formation.

We can no longer see the continued loss of and changes to biodiversity as an issue separate from the core concerns of society.

Increasingly, restoration of terrestrial, inland water and marine ecosystems will be needed to re-establish ecosystem functioning and the provision of valuable services. Economic analysis shows that ecosystem restoration can give good economic rates of return. However the biodiversity and associated services of restored ecosystems usually remain below the levels of natural ecosystems. This reinforces the argument that, where possible, avoiding degradation through conservation is preferable (and even more cost-effective) than restoration after the event.

Government and Business Roles

Better decisions for biodiversity must be made at all levels and in all sectors, in particular the major economic sectors, and government has a key enabling role to play. National programmes or legislation can be crucial in creating a favourable environment to support effective "bottom-up" initiatives led by communities, local authorities, or businesses. This also includes empowering indigenous peoples and local communities to take responsibility for biodiversity management and decision-making; and developing systems to ensure that the benefits arising from access to genetic resources are equitably shared.

We can no longer see the continued loss of and changes to biodiversity as an issue separate from the core concerns of society: to tackle poverty, to improve the health, prosperity and security of our populations, and to deal with climate change. Each of those objectives is undermined by current trends in the state of our ecosystems, and each will be greatly strengthened if we correctly value the role of biodiversity in supporting the shared priorities of the international community. Achieving this will involve placing biodiversity in the mainstream of decision-making in government, the private sector, and other institutions from the local to international scales.

The action taken over the next decade or two, and the direction charted under the Convention on Biological Diversity, will determine whether the relatively stable environmental conditions on which human civilization has depended for the past 10,000 years will continue beyond this century. If we fail to use this opportunity, many ecosystems on the planet will move into new, unprecedented states in which the capacity to provide for the needs of present and future generations is highly uncertain.

Species Loss Is a Silent Crisis for the Planet

David Suzuki

David Suzuki is a prominent scientist, environmentalist, and broadcaster, as well as the cofounder of the David Suzuki Foundation, an environmental conservation organization based in Canada.

Scientists warn that the twin threats of climate change and wildlife extinction threaten our planet's life-support systems, including clean air, clean water, and productive soil. Awareness about the causes and consequences of climate change is growing, leading some governments to look for solutions in areas such as clean energy. Species extinction, however, has gone largely unnoticed by government leaders.

In an article in the *Guardian* newspaper, France's ecology secretary and the World Resources Institute's vice-president of science and research argue that "Unlike the impacts of climate change, biodiversity—and the ecosystem services it harbours—disappears in a mostly silent, local and anonymous fashion. This may explain in part why the devastation of nature has triggered fewer alarm bells than a hotting-up planet."

Sadly, this is true. Unlike the devastating forest fires, deadly heat waves, and violent storms that have ravaged the planet as a result of climate change, the disappearance of plants and animals seems only to get the attention of politicians when it results in serious economic and social upheaval—such as when overfishing led to the collapse of cod stocks in Atlantic Canada, throwing thousands of fishermen out of work.

A Catastrophic Crisis

The unravelling of food webs that have taken millennia to evolve is happening all around us. With every patch of forest cut, wetland drained, or grassland paved over, our actions are destroying wildlife habitat at an unprecedented rate.

Scientists warn that we are in the midst of a human-caused catastrophic wildlife crisis. Of the species we know about, some 17,000 plants and animals are facing extinction, including 12 per cent of birds, nearly a quarter of mammals, and a third of amphibians. Some of the species most vulnerable to human impacts are iconic, well-loved creatures. For example, of the eight distinct bear species that grace our planet, six are now in serious trouble, including sun bears, pandas, and polar bears.

One recent outcome of the global biodiversity talks gives us hope.

The response of our leaders has for the most part been abysmal. The United Nations has declared 2010 the International Year of Biodiversity. Countries are now reporting on their progress in reducing biodiversity loss as required under an international treaty called the Convention on Biological Diversity that most nations, including Canada, have signed. However, the UN has admitted that governments have failed to meet the treaty's objectives "to achieve by 2010 a significant reduction of the current rate of biodiversity loss at the global, regional and national level as a contribution to poverty alleviation and to the benefit of all life on Earth."

A Reason for Hope

Despite our collective failure to meet the 2010 biodiversity target, countries are preparing to negotiate new global targets to slow the rate of biodiversity loss. A flurry of international activity is now underway that will include a special session of the UN General Assembly on the biodiversity crisis in September [2010].

It's easy to be skeptical about the effect these negotiations and meetings in plush hotel ballrooms will have on protecting life on our planet, given the lack of meaningful progress so far. But one recent outcome of the global biodiversity talks gives us hope.

Government negotiators from around the world just met in Busan, South Korea, where they approved the creation of a new global science body that will act as an "early warning system" to inform government leaders on major biodiversity declines and to identify what governments must do to reverse these damaging trends.

This global Biodiversity Scientific Body will be modelled on the Intergovernmental Panel on Climate Change (IPCC), which, through science, has catalyzed world-wide understanding and action on global warming.

Despite the efforts of huge multinational oil companies to discredit its work, the IPCC has compiled the best available science on the causes and impacts of global warming, as well as charting the most effective ways for us to solve the problem. In doing so, it has ensured that climate change has remained a priority for governments, and has proven to be an invaluable tool to help the media understand and report on the issue—independent of politics or PR [public relations] spin. We hope the newly created "IPCC for Nature" will play a similar role in educating, inspiring, and mobilizing policymakers and the public to take decisive action to stem the biodiversity crisis.

Climate Change Is Accelerating Biodiversity Loss

Anup Shah

Anup Shah is the founder of Global Issues, an educational web-site that provides information and analysis about social, politi-cal, economic, and environmental issues that affect the entire planet.

The link between climate change and biodiversity has long been established. Although throughout Earth's history the climate has always changed with ecosystems and species coming and going, *rapid* climate change affects ecosystems and species ability to adapt and so biodiversity loss increases.

A Risk for Human Security

From a human perspective, the rapid climate change and accelerating biodiversity loss risks human security (e.g. a major change in the food chain upon which we depend, water sources may change, recede or disappear, medicines and other resources we rely on may be harder to obtain as the plants and forna they are derived from may reduce or disappear, etc.).

The UN's [United Nations] Global Biodiversity Outlook 3, in May 2010, summarized some concerns that climate change will have on ecosystems:

> Climate change is already having an impact on biodiversity and is projected to become a progressively more significant threat in the coming decades. Loss of Arctic sea ice threatens biodiversity across an entire biome and beyond. The related

pressure of ocean acidification, resulting from higher concentrations of carbon dioxide in the atmosphere, is also already being observed.

Ecosystems are already showing negative impacts under current levels of climate change . . . which is modest compared to future projected changes. . . . In addition to warming temperatures, more frequent extreme weather events and changing patterns of rainfall and drought can be expected to have significant impacts on biodiversity. . . .

Some species may benefit from climate change (including, from a human perspective, an increases in diseases and pests) but the rapid nature of the change suggests that most species will not find it as beneficial as most will not be able to adapt. . . .

Climate Change Impacts on Biodiversity in the Arctic

The Arctic, Antarctic and high latitudes have had the highest rates of warming, and this trend is projected to continue, as the above-mentioned Global Biodiversity Outlook 3 notes.

The iconic polar bear at the top of that food chain is therefore not the only species at risk even though it may get more media attention.

In the Arctic, it is not just a reduction in the extent of sea ice, but its thickness and age. Less ice means less reflective surface meaning more rapid melting. The rapid reduction exceeds even scientific forecasts. . . .

In terms of biodiversity, "the prospect of ice-free summers in the Arctic Ocean implies the loss of an entire biome", the Global Biodiversity Outlook notes.

In addition, "Whole species assemblages are adapted to life on top of or under ice—from the algae that grow on the underside of multi-year ice, forming up to 25% of the Arctic Ocean's primary production, to the invertebrates, birds, fish and marine mammals further up the food chain." The iconic polar bear at the top of that food chain is therefore not the only species at risk even though it may get more media attention.

Note, the ice in the Arctic does thaw and refreeze each year, but it is that pattern which has changed a lot in recent years. . . .

It is also important to note that loss of sea ice has implications on biodiversity beyond the Arctic, as the Global Biodiversity Outlook report also summarizes:

- Bright white ice reflects sunlight.

- When it is replaced by darker water, the ocean and the air heat much faster, a feedback that accelerates ice melt and heating of surface air inland, with resultant loss of tundra.

- Less sea ice leads to changes in seawater temperature and salinity, leading to changes in primary productivity and species composition of plankton and fish, as well as large-scale changes in ocean circulation, affecting biodiversity well beyond the Arctic. . . .

Climate Change Means Ocean Change

When talking about the impacts of climate change, we mostly hear about changes to land and the planet's surface or atmosphere. However, most of the warming is going into the oceans where a lot of ecosystem changes are also occurring:

As John Cook, [the climate communication fellow for the Global Change Institute at the University of Queensland in Australia explains] . . . , "Just as it takes time for a cup of coffee to release heat into the air, so too it takes time for the ocean to release its heat into the atmosphere."

Indeed, . . . the warming in the oceans has been occurring for quite some time. . . .

The implications of this is further explained with *Inter Press Service's* freezer analogy: The world's northern freezer is on rapid defrost as large volumes of warm water are pouring into the Arctic Ocean, speeding the melt of sea ice. . . .

Ove Hoegh-Guldberg, [the director of Australia's Global Change Institute] talks about the impact climate change will have on ocean ecosystems. . . :

> Rapidly rising greenhouse gas concentrations are driving ocean systems toward conditions not seen for millions of years, with an associated risk of fundamental and irreversible ecological transformation. Changes in biological function in the ocean caused by anthropogenic climate change go far beyond death, extinctions and habitat loss: fundamental processes are being altered, community assemblages are being reorganized and ecological surprises are likely.

Increasing Ocean Acidification

Although it has gained less mainstream media attention, the effects of increasing greenhouse emissions—in particular carbon dioxide—on the oceans may well be significant.

Although millions of years ago CO_2 levels were higher, today's change is occurring rapidly, giving many marine organisms too little time to adapt.

As explained by the US agency, the National Oceanic and Atmospheric Administration (NOAA), the basic chemistry of ocean acidification is well understood.

These are the 3 main concepts:

1. More CO_2 [carbon dioxide] in the atmosphere means more CO_2 in the ocean

2. Atmospheric CO_2 is dissolved in the ocean, which becomes more acidic; and

3. The resulting changes in the chemistry of the oceans disrupt the ability of plants and animals in the sea to make shells and skeletons of calcium carbonate while dissolving shells already formed.

Scientists have found that oceans are able to absorb some of the excess CO_2 released by human activity. This has helped keep the planet cooler than it otherwise could have been had these gases remained in the atmosphere.

However, the additional *excess* CO_2 being absorbed is also resulting in the acidification of the oceans: When CO_2 reacts with water it produces a weak acid called carbonic acid, changing the sea water chemistry. As the Global Biodiversity Outlook report explains, the water is some 30% more acidic than pre-industrial times, depleting carbonate ions—the building blocks for many marine organisms. In addition, concentrations of carbonate ions are now lower than at any time during the last 800,000 years. The impacts on ocean biological diversity and ecosystem functioning will likely be severe, though the precise timing and distribution of these impacts are uncertain.

Although millions of years ago CO_2 levels were higher, today's change is occurring rapidly, giving many marine organisms too little time to adapt. Some marine creatures are growing thinner shells or skeletons, for example. Some of these creatures play a crucial role in the food chain, and in ecosystem biodiversity.

Some species may benefit from the extra carbon dioxide, and a few years ago scientists and organizations, such as the European Project on OCean Acidification, formed to try to understand and assess the impacts further.

One example of recent findings is a tiny sand grain-sized plankton responsible for the sequestration of 25–50% of the carbon the oceans absorb is affected by increasing ocean acidification. This tiny plankton plays a major role in keeping atmospheric carbon dioxide (CO_2) concentrations at much lower levels than they would be otherwise so large effects on them could be quite serious.

Other related problems reported by the *Inter Press Service* [IPS] include more oceanic dead zones (areas where there is too little oxygen in the sea to support life) and the decline of important coastal plants and forests, such as mangrove forests that play an important role in carbon absorption. This is on top of the already declining ocean biodiversity that has been happening for a few decades, now.

Increasing Ocean Stratification

As climate change warms the oceans (even just an increase of about 0.2C per decade, on average), the warmer water (which is lighter) tends to stay on top of what is then a layer of colder water.

This affects tiny drifting marine organisms known as phytoplankton. Though small, "Phytoplankton are a critical part of our planetary life support system. They produce half of the oxygen we breathe, draw down surface CO_2, and ultimately support all of our fisheries," says Boris Worm of Canada's Dalhousie University and one of the world's leading experts on the global oceans. . . .

Phytoplankton can only live in the top 100 or 200 meters of water, but if it is getting warmer, they eventually run out of nutrients to feed on unless the cold, deeper waters mix with those near the surface.

Ocean stratification has been widely observed in the past decade and is occurring in more and larger areas of the world's oceans.

Researchers have found a direct correlation between rising sea surface temperatures and the decline in phytoplankton growth around the world.

As NASA [National Aeronautics and Space Administration] summarizes, stratification cuts down the amount of carbon the ocean can take up.

Increasing Oceanic Dead Zones

The past half-century has seen an explosive growth in aquatic dead zones, areas too low in dissolved oxygen to support life. . . .

Around the world, coral reefs have been dying largely due to climate change.

Fertilizer and sewage run-off cause huge growth of plankton. However, these then quickly die and are consumed by bacteria that deplete waters of oxygen. For example, the Gulf of Mexico has a 22,000 square kilometer dead zone every spring due to run-off from the Mississippi River.

There is also a linkage with climate change. [As environmental reporter Stephen Leahy writes:]

> Ocean stratification, where warm water sits firmly on top of cold, nutrient-rich water, also creates dead zones and lowers the overall productivity of the oceans. . . . Such dead zones were rare 40 years ago but now number several hundred. Without urgent action, climate change will continue to warm oceans, increasing stratification and producing larger and more dead zones with a major impact on future fisheries, a 2009 study in Nature Geoscience warned.

> It will take a thousand years for the oceans to cool down, so it is imperative to pull the emergency brake on global warming emissions, the study concluded.

Coral Reefs Threatened by Climate Change

Around the world, coral reefs have been dying largely due to climate change.

At the beginning of September, 2009, the Australian agency looking after the Great Barrier Reef released an outlook report warning the Great Barrier Reef is in trouble.

But it is not just the Great Barrier Reef at risk. All of them are at risk, says Charlie Veron, an Australian marine biologist who is widely regarded as the world's foremost expert on coral reefs.

"The future is horrific", he says. "There is no hope of reefs surviving to even mid-century in any form that we now recognize. If, and when, they go, they will take with them about one-third of the world's marine biodiversity. Then there is a domino effect, as reefs fail so will other ecosystems. This is the path of a mass extinction event, when most life, especially tropical marine life, goes extinct."

Coral reefs provide many ecosystem services to humans as well, for free. . . .

Lizards Threatened by Climate Change

What the *BBC* described as a "global-scale study" published in the journal *Science* found that climate change could wipe out 20% of the world's lizard species by 2080.

Global projection models used by the scientists suggested that "lizards have already crossed a threshold for extinctions caused by climate change".

The fear of lowland species moving to higher elevations has long been predicted as an effect of climate change. This has been observed with lizard populations too, as the leader of the research team told the *BBC*: "We are actually seeing lowland species moving upward in elevation, slowly driving upland species extinct, and if the upland species can't evolve fast enough then they're going to continue to go extinct."

Why are lizards so sensitive to climate change? The *BBC* summarizes:

> Lizards, the researchers say, are far more susceptible to climate-warming extinction than previously thought. Many species live right at the edge of their "thermal limits".

Rising temperatures, they explained, leave lizards unable to spend sufficient time foraging for food, as they have to rest and regulate their body temperature.

The above areas of biodiversity affected is by no means exhaustive. Other areas affected by climate change include terrestrial animals, and forests, water sources and related ecologies, and so on.

Biodiversity Loss Is a Threat to Human Food Security

Paul Virgo

Paul Virgo is a freelance journalist based in Rome who regularly writes for Reuters, a global news agency, as well as other publications.

When people talk about biodiversity loss, discussion often centres on the tragedy of animals like the tiger and the panda being in danger of extinction.

It is as if the world were about to be deprived of precious parts of its heritage, perhaps comparable to works by Mozart or Shakespeare—sad yet not something that will affect our everyday existence.

Unfortunately, this widely held vision is misguided.

Biodiversity loss is a massive threat to human food security and, ultimately, to our species' survival as well as to that of the millions of plants, animals and bacteria which share the planet with us.

"Biodiversity loss is not just a question of landscapes and species protection, it's also about agricultural issues upon which we rely to grow our food," Marco Contiero of [the environmental group] Greenpeace told IPS [Inter Press Service]. "It's about us."

Biodiversity, Climate Change, and Food Security

The Rome-based Bioversity International research institute has organised a week of events in the run-up to Saturday's [May 22, 2010] World Biodiversity Day—in 2010, the United Nations International Year of Biodiversity—and one of its main objectives is to highlight the link between agricultural biodiversity and food security in a context of climate change.

Having a variety of crops in a field gives farmers an "insurance policy", as it raises the chances that at least part of the harvest will be able to withstand the stresses that arrive.

The biggest problem climate change is expected to cause for food security is a predicted increase in extreme weather, which will put crops under a number of different stresses. This means that even if technology gives farmers a solution to one stress, for example with a genetically-modified drought-resistant organism, this crop is in danger of failing when faced with another, such as excessive rainfall or an unseasonably cold snap.

To make matters worse, climate change is expected to hit hardest in areas already highly exposed to food insecurity, such as sub-Saharan Africa and southern Asia.

Biodiversity Helps Improve Food Security

But biodiversity can provide the answer in various ways, experts say.

Firstly, having a variety of crops in a field gives farmers an 'insurance policy', as it raises the chances that at least part of the harvest will be able to withstand the stresses that arrive, something that is not the case with industrial monoculture farming.

This might mean that farmers produce less in one particular year, but it should ensure higher output over the medium term, according to several studies.

Species diversity also reduces the threat of pests and diseases, simply by diluting the availability of the potential hosts, and improves soil fertility, therefore reducing the need for expensive and environmentally damaging herbicides, pesticides and fertilisers.

It is important for the nutritional side of food security too.

The U.N. [United Nations] Food and Agriculture Organisation [FAO] says that over one billion people are hungry, three-quarters of whom are rural poor in developing countries, but the number who are malnourished because of poor diets is a lot higher.

"Poor farmers don't have any reserves and biodiversity is the main tool they have to manage risk. So we need to look at a very different approach to agricultural diversification, one that is based on the use of diversity," Bioversity International's director general Emile Frison told IPS.

"There are multiple benefits that can be derived from this, not just from a point of view of a more sustainable agriculture, but also in terms of the advantages of having diverse agriculture, which leads to diverse diet. This is essential for good nutrition and health. This is becoming an extremely important problem in many developing countries."

And, crucially, crop diversity also enables farmers to see which plants adapt best to changing climatic conditions and adjust their practises to evolve with the local impacts of the greenhouse effect.

This is why reversing biodiversity loss is not just an imperative for the two billion people in developing countries whose livelihoods depend on smallholder farms.

The Vulnerable Global Food System

While biodiversity faces many threats, including urbanization, deforestation and pollution, possibly the biggest drivers of its reduction are agricultural modernization and simplification of diets.

These have led to the current state of affairs in which the FAO says a dozen species provides 90 percent of the animal protein consumed globally and just four crop species provide half of plant-based calories in the human diet.

As a result the food supplies of the well-fed populations of developed countries are increasingly vulnerable too, as agriculture has fewer and fewer resources with which to adapt to environmental challenges, such as climate change and water scarcity.

"Studies show that if we keep losing biodiversity at the same pace as now, by 2050 we'll be confronted with an economic cost equal to 14 trillion euros," Contiero said.

With FAO estimating that about three-quarters of the genetic diversity of agricultural crops has been lost over the last century, many believe the time has come for a radical change in the way we produce our food.

"We need to have a different paradigm of agriculture, one that is not based on the fixed reduction of the agricultural model, which is what has been done with industrial agriculture, to one that is based on diversity," said Frison.

There is still room for optimism, largely because smallholder farmers in developing countries are watching over much of the rich biodiversity that, despite everything, still exists.

Therefore, the developed world should perhaps find ways to encourage them to continue doing this precious job, not just to help pull them out of hunger and poverty, but also out of self-interest.

Kanayo Nwanze, president of the U.N. rural poverty agency the International Fund for Agricultural Development (IFAD), said this week: "Poor rural people and their communities are not only dependent on agricultural biodiversity, but also they are important custodians of it."

Rainforest Regrowth May Reduce the Loss of Biodiversity in the Tropics

Environment News Service

Environment News Service is a daily international online wire service that provides late-breaking environmental news.

Vast stretches of abandoned tropical forests that were once logged or farmed are regrowing, prompting an international debate among scientists meeting at the Smithsonian's National Museum of Natural History today [January 12, 2009]. At issue is the extent to which this rainforest regrowth might reduce the loss of biodiversity.

The Rainforest Debate

Scientists have predicted that up to half of all species may be lost in our lifetimes. But some researchers contend that rainforest regrowth has not been adequately factored into estimates of future species loss and that the biodiversity crisis has been overstated.

Others maintain that only 50 to 80 percent of plant species may return to logged or altered forests, and many animal species will not survive the transition.

Still others warn that the continuing rapid expansion of logging and mining roads makes forest access easier for commercial poachers and hungry people. Animals are being hunted for exotic food, trophies, medicine and pets on levels that threaten the continued existence of many species, they argue.

This increasing harvest of animals, combined with the emergence of devastating wildlife diseases, habitat loss due to industrial scale development, climate change and other factors, is a recipe for catastrophic biodiversity collapse, despite encouraging evidence of rainforest regrowth, says this group of scientists.

Deforestation and Land Abandonment

The need to explore these issues has prompted the Smithsonian to invite experts to present their ideas at today's symposium on the tropical extinction crisis.

Cristian Samper, director of the National Museum of Natural History, said, "By bringing together the world's foremost authorities on different aspects of rainforest science, we hope to achieve new insights into a situation with potentially profound implications for all species, ours included."

Once the land is abandoned, the regrowth is relatively quick. . . . The forest canopy closes after 15 years. After 20 years, about half of the original biomass weight has grown back.

Symposium presenter Greg Asner of the Carnegie Institution says the tropics originally had almost 20 million square kilometers of rainforests. Today's best available but rough estimates, based on a combination of satellite data and field research, show:

- 10 million square kilometers have been cleared of at least half their forest cover for human use

- 5 million square kilometers have been selectively logged, often with high-impact methods that leave forests degraded

- Of the intact forest remaining, about 275,000 square kilometers were clear-cut in the five years from 2000 to 2005

- 350,000 square kilometers, or 1.7 percent of the original forested area, are in some stage of regrowth today, most in south Asia and Latin America

According to Asner and others, deforestation is the most profound change underway in tropical rainforests, but land abandonment is the second most important trend.

Often the inhabitants of upland areas that offered marginal farming opportunities leave to pursue better income opportunities in lowlands and cities.

Once the land is abandoned, the regrowth is relatively quick, scientists have found. The forest canopy closes after 15 years. After 20 years, about half of the original biomass weight has grown back.

The symposium is co-chaired by William Laurance and S. Joseph Wright of the Smithsonian Tropical Research Institute based in Panama. The two scientists authored differing papers in academic journals that sparked much of this scientific controversy.

Wright notes that over 20 percent of all land within 10 degrees of the Equator now has protected status, and that the tropics have a percentage of protected land greater than North America, Europe or Japan.

The world now loses the equivalent of 50 football fields of old-growth forest every minute.

The impact of climate change on tropical biodiversity is his primary concern today, but Wright believes that forested areas will never fall to the lowest levels predicted. He says extinction will threaten a smaller proportion of tropical forest species than predicted.

This position is based in part on United Nations predictions of growing urbanization and slower population growth as mid-century approaches.

But Laurance argues that secondary and degraded forests will sustain only a fraction of existing animal species. He notes that birds and mammals are more vulnerable to the altered habitat than insects and other small organisms.

The world now loses the equivalent of 50 football fields of old-growth forest every minute, he says. "Rainforest regrowth is indeed occurring in regions but most old growth is destroyed."

The Impact of Hunting

Symposium speaker Elizabeth Bennett, director of hunting and wildlife trade for the New York-based Wildlife Conservation Society, says access for hunters to tens of thousands of square kilometers of virgin rainforests worldwide is being created annually and huge regions are being virtually drained of wildlife.

"Hunting has long been known as a primary cause of wildlife species depletion in tropical forests," she says. "Logging companies frequently regard wild meat as a free subsidy to feed their workers."

The "empty forest syndrome" affecting much of Asia and Africa is spreading rapidly to other parts of the tropical forest world, she says.

Bennett points to the recent seizure of two shipments of scaly anteaters from Sumatra bound for China where they are used to make soup. Fourteen tons seized were in Sumatra, Indonesia and 23 tons seized in Vietnam, more than 7,000 animals in total.

In Vietnam alone, 12 species of large animals have gone extinct, or virtually extinct, in the past 50 years mainly due to hunting, she says.

The chytrid fungus, meanwhile, has wiped out hundreds of amphibian species worldwide.

Disease can compound the impact of hunting. The Ebola virus, for example, has reduced gorilla populations in northwest Congo by up to 95 percent, chimpanzee populations by an estimated 83 percent and threatens great ape populations elsewhere in Central Africa.

Says Bennett, "The implications of all this for loss of ecosystem function are still not fully understood, although many studies show that tropical forests depleted of large vertebrates experience reduced seed dispersal, altered patterns of tree recruitment and shifts in the relative abundances of species.

"The loss of top predators and other 'keystone species' has a disproportionate impact on ecosystems and can result in dramatic biodiversity changes."

Linking Old Growth and New Forests

Thomas Rudel of Rutgers University says rainforest destruction is no longer small-scale but industrial large-scale. He suggests working in a more focused way with managers of large natural resource corporations operating in tropical countries and supports certification programs that identify products produced under sustainable conditions.

Robin Chazdon of the University of Connecticut told the symposium that biological corridors between remnants of old-growth forest and patches of younger forests and agroforests will enhanc[e] their role as arks to protect species.

"If we can protect, expand and enhance forest cover in these altered landscapes," Chazdon says, "the prognosis for conserving many forms of plant and animal life will improve in many regions."

Animal and Plant Extinction Rates May Be Overestimated

Brian Handwerk

Brian Handwerk is a regular correspondent, and a former pro-ducer, for National Geographic News, *an online news magazine published by the National Geographic Society, a nonprofit scien-tific and educational institution devoted to geography, archaeol-ogy, and the promotion of environmental and historical conser-vation.*

Global extinction rates may have been overestimated by as much as 160 percent, according to a new analysis.

In recent decades numerous studies have predicted that habitat destruction will doom some 20 to 50 percent of Earth's species within 500 years.

It's true that many species are still dying off, but the de-cline is happening at a slower pace than generally feared, ac-cording to study co-author Stephen Hubbell, an ecologist at the University of California, Los Angeles.

"The good news is that we may have a little more time in terms of saving some species," Hubbell said.

The bad news, he stressed, is that surging extinctions driven by habitat loss remain the critical conservation prob-lem of the 21st century.

Method for Measuring Extinctions Flawed?

There's no proven, direct method for verifying extinction rates, so most scientists have relied on an indirect method to estimate how quickly plants and animals are disappearing.

That method calculates the rate at which new species are found when a new habitat area is sampled—called the species-area relationship (SAR)—and simply reverses that curve to predict the number of species that will go extinct as similarly sized areas of habitat are destroyed.

But Hubbell said the method is flawed, because much more land area must be lost to cause an extinction than is required to find a new species.

That's because only one individual of a species needs to be found in an area for scientists to deem it a new population, but extinction requires every member of a species to disappear.

The scientists calculated that the [species-area relationship]-derived extinction rates had been overstated by as much as 160 percent.

"It's equivalent to saying a species is committed to extinction if you find the first individual and destroy its habitat, and that's clearly not true," Hubbell said.

"You have to destroy all of the habitat that has all the individuals of a species in it before that species goes extinct."

Hubbell and colleague Fangliang He of Sun Yat-sen University in Guangzhou, China, analyzed data from eight previously mapped forest areas from around the world. Each plot was between about 50 and 125 acres (20 and 50 hectares). The team also looked at ranges of several bird species in the continental United States.

Based on this real-life data and a mathematical model—in which the hypothetical destruction of habitat always resulted in fewer extinctions than predicted by SAR—the scientists calculated that the SAR-derived extinction rates had been overstated by as much as 160 percent.

The team also suggested that future studies could reveal even higher overestimates in some places.

Habitat Loss Still a Threat to Species

Yet ecologist Eric Dinerstein, who wasn't involved in the new study, said that examining how extinction rates are calculated is a bit of an academic argument for many conservationists.

"If it's a 160 percent overestimate or an 80 percent overestimate or a 20 percent overestimate, [comparing] which model of extinction rates is more accurate isn't the most important question," said Dinerstein, vice president of conservation science for WWF, a global conservation group.

"The overpowering message is that habitat loss and fragmentation are still the greatest threat to the future of species, and they are only increasing."

Dinerstein added that it's hard to determine when a species has gone extinct, as evidenced by numerous animals once thought gone but later found alive in small numbers.

And the final extinction of a species may be beside the point, Dinerstein said. What really matters is ecological extinction.

[The new] research doesn't change the big picture, which isn't particularly rosy for species survival.

"That's when a population drops below a certain number of individuals and is no longer playing an ecological role in the ecosystem," Dinerstein said.

At this point the diminished species has so little interaction with the other plants and animals in the habitat that the species might as well be gone, from the point of view of the ecosystem.

Ecological extinction is of "much more concern to conservationists than [identifying] the last one or two individuals of some species which are still [alive] but functionally extinct."

Extinction Rates Critical for Conservation

Hubbell and He stressed that their research doesn't change the big picture, which isn't particularly rosy for species survival.

"I think [scientists and conservationists] are right in saying that we're really on the cusp of a sixth mass extinction or that it's actually in progress. We certainly don't disagree with that assessment," said Hubbell, whose study appears May 19 [2011] in the journal *Nature*.

But he also noted that learning how to calculate extinction rates properly is critical for conservation.

Take extinction-rate estimates by major initiatives, such as the Intergovernmental Panel on Climate Change reports and the U.N.'s [United Nations] Millennium Ecosystem Assessment.

If such estimates "are going to have consequences for billions of dollars in conservation efforts, don't you think we ought to know better why we're spending money and what the actual numbers are?" Hubbell said.

Co-author He also told reporters during a press briefing that no other scientific activity is arguably more important than understanding the causes and consequences of species extinctions.

However, He and Hubbell added that determining extinction rates has a long way to go.

"The bad news is that we really don't have good methods for estimating extinction yet," Hubbell explained.

"The precise answer depends on the precise pattern of habitat destruction in relation to the precise distribution of species.

"And although we can look at habitat destruction from satellites, we often just don't know where species live on the ground."

Environmentalists' Claims About Species' Loss Are Radically Misleading

James D. Agresti

James D. Agresti is a conservative/libertarian writer and the president of Just Facts, a nonprofit research and education institute dedicated to researching, documenting, and publishing information on public policy issues.

"Overall, species loss is now occurring at a rate 1,000 times greater than the natural background rate," says [former Vice President] Al Gore in the Academy Award-winning documentary *An Inconvenient Truth*. However, new data published in a peer-reviewed journal illustrate how this claim . . . is radically misleading.

Gore fails to mention that this "natural background rate" he speaks of is a fossil-based estimate burdened with so many assumptions that a 2005 Cambridge University Press book on biodiversity states that no "serious" attempt has been made to "judge the reliability" of this figure. Indeed, the "uncertainties at each stage of the calculation" would make the effort worthless. The book goes on to explain, "Probably no one will be surprised if this estimate is off by a factor of 10 or even 100."

The Implausibility of Gore's Numbers

To illustrate the vacuousness of comparing modern extinction rates to the so-called background extinction rate, we need only to apply Gore's "1,000 times" claim to some hard data, which we can find in a recently published paper in the journal *Diversity and Distributions*. The authors of this paper analyzed the "actual historical record of extinctions" and found that a total of 190 birds and land-dwelling mammals have gone extinct since the year 1500.

Consequently, if humans were causing these species to disappear at 1,000 times the natural rate, in the absence of man, one-fifth (190/1,000) of a single bird or mammal would have gone extinct in the past five hundred years. These figures become even more implausible when we consider the fact that only nine of these 190 extinct species lived on continents. The rest lived on islands, where populations are small and geographically restricted, causing them to be poorly represented in the fossil record and hence inapplicable to the background extinction rate.

Thus, here is the more significant fact: if continental birds and mammals were actually going extinct at 1,000 times the natural rate, in the absence of man's influence, only one continental bird or mammal would go extinct every 56,000 years. This absurd result shows just how far-fetched Gore's assertion is. Furthermore, as the paper's authors point out, mammals "are widely assumed to be at greater risk [of extinction] than other species."

Note that Gore is not the only environmentalist to paint such a dire and distorted picture of modern man causing wholesale extinctions. Michael J. Novacek of the American Museum of Natural History wrote in a 2007 book that "species are going extinct at thousands of times the background extinction rate" and that we are "thus likely to lose 30 to 50 percent of all living species within this century." Contrast this wild claim with the data in the above-cited paper, which shows:

> The three extinct mammals represent approximately 0.08% of the continental species pool. Even if we assume that all three went extinct in the past 100 years (vs. 500 year), it would take, at this rate, 1235 years for 1% of continental mammals to go extinct. Similarly for birds, the six species

represent 0.062% of the 9672 species pool and it would take 1613 years to lose 1% of extant species at current rates even if the recorded extinctions all took place over the last 100 years.

Other Misleading Gore Claims

An interesting aside arose during a presentation I gave this week before the Manhattan Libertarian Party. An astute audience member noticed that one of the creatures in Gore's graphic of extinct species is a coelacanth, which is a fish that isn't actually extinct. Coelacanths were alleged to have disappeared 65–70 million years ago, but in 1938, a fisherman caught one off the coast of South Africa. Since then, more than 170 living coelacanths have been pulled from the waters. . . .

By my count, there are more than 25 inaccurate or misleading claims in *An Inconvenient Truth*, yet the *Associated Press* reports that 19 of our "nation's top climate scientists" gave it "five stars for accuracy." Moreover, the film is being shown in schools throughout the world, and five nations have made it an official part of their educational curricula. Thus, if you know an audience that wants to understand the inconvenient facts about *An Inconvenient Truth*, I am currently available for presentations.

CHAPTER 2

Which Plant and Animal Species Are Threatened with Extinction?

Chapter Preface

O ne sign of biodiversity loss, some scientists say, is a marked decline of honeybees—a type of bee used around the world to pollinate crops and plants. Significant reductions in the numbers of honeybees was first seen in the United States and Europe during the first decade of the twenty-first century, but as of 2012 researchers now are observing signs of similar bee collapses in China, Japan, and Egypt, suggesting it is a global phenomenon. Scientists studying the problem have not reached a definitive explanation for why this is happening, but many experts think there may be a number of factors at play, many of them linked to a decline in overall biodiversity. The bee decline is alarming, experts say, because bees are considered to be a keystone species—that is, a species important for the functioning of many other species and ecosystems due to their role as pollinators of flowering plants. Without bees, numerous plant and animal species in tropical forests and woodlands throughout the world would not survive, and the commercial production of crops that produce seeds, nuts, berries, and fruits—which are dependent on bee pollination—would be destroyed.

The role of bees as pollinators is well-known. Pollination basically is the transfer of pollen—a powdery substance produced by plants for fertilization—from the anther (the male part of the flower) to the stigma (the female part of the flower). According to the Food and Agriculture Organization of the United Nations (FAO), around 80 percent of flowering plants depend on insect pollination to reproduce, and bees are the major insect pollinators. About half of the pollinators of tropical plants, for example, are bees. Bees do this work by foraging into and around flowering plants looking for nectar—a substance produced by the plants that bees eat as food. Plants have evolved so that the bees, while searching for food, must brush up against the flowers' anthers, which are covered with pollen. The bodies of bees are covered with hairs that catch the pollen, and as the bees fly from flower to flower, they deliver the pollen to the next flower's stigma, achieving pollination. Although some plants require multiple bee visits to acquire enough pollen grains to reproduce, pollination is the first step in the plant fertilization process. Once it is adequately pollinated, the plant then is able to produce seeds, nuts, or fruits that can eventually create a new plant.

The value of bee pollination to humans is also beyond question. According to the FAO, over seventy of the one hundred agricultural crops that provide 90 percent of the world's food are reliant on bee pollination. Bees also provide wax for cosmetics and honey. Although there are many species of bees, in the United States the main crop pollinator is the honeybee. Some estimates say that honeybee pollination of major US crops—including fruits, vegetables, nuts, and livestock feeds—is worth about $15 billion annually. California's almond crop, for example, which makes up 80 percent of the world's almond supply, represents about $2 billion of this amount and is completely dependent on honeybees. Honeybees also pollinate many wild plants in the United States, helping to protect native biodiversity.

Other species of bees are similarly critical to agriculture and wild ecosystems in other countries. In Brazil, for example, a bee species called Euglossa is the main pollinator for the Brazil nut tree—a tree that grows wild in the Amazon forest that produces Brazil nuts, one of the country's main export crops. And in addition, bees are vitally important in wild forest ecosystems around the world, particularly European deciduous forests, where the floors are covered by flowering plants that require quick pollination by bees before the trees produce their leaves. Bees also pollinate a number of trees, bushes, and other plants that produce berries, seeds, and fruits eaten by wild animals and birds.

Scientists have been studying the problem of bee decline for many years, but no single cause has been identified. A 2011 report from the United Nations Environment Program (UNEP) concluded that a number of factors may be combining to cause bee die-offs. These include: habitat loss (including the loss of flowering plants that provide food for bees); the overuse of insecticides that may be present in the nectar eaten by bees; an increase in bee parasites and pests; and air pollution that may be limiting the distance that flower scents can travel, making it harder for bees to find flowering plants. Other researchers suggest that honeybee decline may be caused by reduced plant diversity because wild flowering plants are also declining. This research has found that bees fed with the nectar of a variety of flowers have stronger immune systems than those reliant on a single flower. Bees, therefore, might have less diversity in their diets than in the past, weakening their immune systems and making them more susceptible to pests and diseases. Bees, however, are only one species under threat today. The authors of the viewpoints in this chapter identify many other plant and animal species that appear to be at risk, and they discuss the rate and causes of species extinctions.

Half of Earth's Species Could Be Extinct by the End of the Century in a Sixth Mass Extinction Event

The Independent

The Independent *is a British national morning newspaper published daily in London.*

Mankind may have unleashed the sixth known mass extinction in Earth's history, according to a paper released on Wednesday [March 2, 2011] by the science journal *Nature*.

Over the past 540 million years, five mega-wipeouts of species have occurred through naturally-induced events.

But the new threat is man-made, inflicted by habitation loss, over-hunting, over-fishing, the spread of germs and viruses and introduced species and by climate change caused by fossil-fuel greenhouse gases, says the study.

A Sixth Mass Extinction

Evidence from fossils suggests that in the "Big Five" extinctions, at least 75 percent of all animal species were destroyed.

Palaeobiologists at the University of California at Berkeley looked at the state of biodiversity today, using the world's mammal species as a barometer.

Until mankind's big expansion some 500 years ago, mammal extinctions were very rare: on average, just two species died out every million years.

But in the last five centuries, at least 80 out of 5,570 mammal species have bitten the dust, providing a clear warning of the peril to biodiversity.

"It looks like modern extinction rates resemble mass extinction rates, even after setting a high bar for defining 'mass extinction,'" said researcher Anthony Bamosky.

Four of the "Big Five" events unfolded on scales estimated at hundreds of thousands to millions of years, inflicted in the main by naturally-caused global warming or cooling.

This picture is supported by the outlook for mammals in the "critically endangered" and "currently threatened" categories of the Red List of biodiversity compiled by the International Union for Conservation of Nature (IUCN).

On the assumption that these species are wiped out and biodiversity loss continues unchecked, "the sixth mass extinction could arrive within as little as three to 22 centuries," said Barnosky.

Compared with nearly all the previous extinctions this would be fast-track.

Four of the "Big Five" events unfolded on scales estimated at hundreds of thousands to millions of years, inflicted in the main by naturally-caused global warming or cooling.

The most abrupt extinction came at the end of the Cretaceous, some 65 million years ago when a comet or asteroid slammed into the Yucatan peninsula, in modern-day Mexico, causing firestorms whose dust cooled the planet.

An estimated 76 percent of species were killed, including the dinosaurs.

The authors admitted to weaknesses in the study. They acknowledged that the fossil record is far from complete, that mammals provide an imperfect benchmark of Earth's biodiversity and further work is needed to confirm their suspicions.

But they described their estimates as conservative and warned a large-scale extinction would have an impact on a timescale beyond human imagining.

"Recovery of biodiversity will not occur on any timeframe meaningful to people," said the study.

"Evolution of new species typically takes at least hundreds of thousands of years, and recovery from mass extinction episodes probably occurs on timescales encompassing millions of years."

Room for Hope

Even so, they stressed, there is room for hope.

"So far, only one to two percent of all species have gone extinct in the groups we can look at clearly, so by those numbers, it looks like we are not far down the road to extinction. We still have a lot of Earth's biota to save," Barnosky said.

Even so, "it's very important to devote resources and legislation toward species conservation if we don't want to be the species whose activity caused a mass extinction."

Asked for an independent comment, French biologist Gilles Boeuf, president of the Museum of Natural History in Paris, said the question of a new extinction was first raised in 2002.

So far, scientists have identified 1.9 million species, and between 16,000 and 18,000 new ones, essentially microscopic, are documented each year.

"At this rate, it will take us a thousand years to record all of Earth's biodiversity, which is probably between 15 and 30 million species" said Boeuf.

"But at the rate things are going, by the end of this century, we may well have wiped out half of them, especially in tropical forests and coral reefs."

Thousands of Plant and Animal Extinctions Are Happening Faster than New Species Can Evolve

Juliette Jowit

Juliette Jowit is a senior journalist at The Guardian, *a British national daily newspaper. She specializes in environmental issues.*

For the first time since the dinosaurs disappeared, humans are driving animals and plants to extinction faster than new species can evolve, one of the world's experts on biodiversity has warned.

Conservation experts have already signalled that the world is in the grip of the "sixth great extinction" of species, driven by the destruction of natural habitats, hunting, the spread of alien predators and disease, and climate change.

However until recently it has been hoped that the rate at which new species were evolving could keep pace with the loss of diversity of life.

Speaking in advance of two reports next week [March 2010] on the state of wildlife in Britain and Europe, Simon Stuart, chair of the Species Survival Commission for the International Union for the Conservation of Nature [IUCN]—the body which officially declares species threatened and extinct—said that point had now "almost certainly" been crossed.

"Measuring the rate at which new species evolve is difficult, but there's no question that the current extinction rates are faster than that; I think it's inevitable," said Stuart.

Today's Extinction Rates

The IUCN created shock waves with its major assessment of the world's biodiversity in 2004, which calculated that the rate of extinction had reached 100–1,000 times that suggested by the fossil records before humans.

Extinction is part of the constant evolution of life, and only 2–4% of the species that have ever lived on Earth are thought to be alive today.

No formal calculations have been published since, but conservationists agree the rate of loss has increased since then, and Stuart said it was possible that the dramatic predictions of experts like the renowned Harvard biologist E O Wilson, that the rate of loss could reach 10,000 times the background rate in two decades, could be correct.

"All the evidence is he's right," said Stuart. "Some people claim it already is that . . . things can only have deteriorated because of the drivers of the losses, such as habitat loss and climate change, all getting worse. But we haven't measured extinction rates again since 2004 and because our current estimates contain a tenfold range there has to be a very big deterioration or improvement to pick up a change."

Extinction is part of the constant evolution of life, and only 2–4% of the species that have ever lived on Earth are thought to be alive today. However fossil records suggest that for most of the planet's 3.5bn [billion] year history the steady rate of loss of species is thought to be about one in every million species each year.

Only 869 extinctions have been formally recorded since 1500, however, because scientists have only "described" nearly 2m [million] of an estimated 5–30m species around the world, and only assessed the conservation status of 3% of those, the global rate of extinction is extrapolated from the rate of loss among species which are known. In this way the IUCN calculated in 2004 that the rate of loss had risen to 100–1,000 per millions species annually—a situation comparable to the five previous "mass extinctions"—the last of which was when the dinosaurs were wiped out about 65m years ago.

An Underestimate of the Problem

Critics, including *The Skeptical Environmentalist* author, Bjørn Lomborg, have argued that because such figures rely on so many estimates of the number of underlying species and the past rate of extinctions based on fossil records of marine animals, the huge margins for error make these figures too unreliable to form the basis of expensive conservation actions.

However Stuart said that the IUCN figure was likely to be an underestimate of the problem, because scientists are very reluctant to declare species extinct even when they have sometimes not been seen for decades, and because few of the world's plants, fungi and invertebrates have yet been formally recorded and assessed.

Nearly 17,300 species are considered under threat. . . . This includes one-in-five mammals assessed, one-in-eight birds, one-in-three amphibians, and one-in-four corals.

The calculated increase in the extinction rate should also be compared to another study of thresholds of resilience for the natural world by Swedish scientists, who warned that anything over 10 times the background rate of extinction—10 species in every million per year—was above the limit that could be tolerated if the world was to be safe for humans, said Stuart.

"No one's claiming it's as small as 10 times," he said. "There are uncertainties all the way down; the only thing we're certain about is the extent is way beyond what's natural and it's getting worse."

Many more species are "discovered" every year around the world, than are recorded extinct, but these "new" plants and animals are existing species found by humans for the first time, not newly evolved species.

In addition to extinctions, the IUCN has listed 208 species as "possibly extinct", some of which have not been seen for decades. Nearly 17,300 species are considered under threat, some in such small populations that only successful conservation action can stop them from becoming extinct in future. This includes one-in-five mammals assessed, one-in-eight birds, one-in-three amphibians, and one-in-four corals.

Conserving Biodiversity

Later this year the Convention on Biological Diversity is expected to formally declare that the pledge by world leaders in 2002 to reduce the rate of biodiversity loss by 2010 has not been met, and to agree new, stronger targets.

Despite the worsening problem, and the increasing threat of climate change, experts stress that understanding of the problems which drive plants and animals to extinction has improved greatly, and that targeted conservation can be successful in saving species from likely extinction in the wild.

This year [2010] has been declared the International Year of Biodiversity and it is also hoped that a major UN [United Nations] report this summer, on the economics of ecosystems and biodiversity, will encourage governments to devote more funds to conservation.

Professor Norman MacLeod, keeper of palaeontology at the Natural History Museum in London, cautioned that when fossil experts find evidence of a great extinction it can appear in a layer of rock covering perhaps 10,000 years, so they cannot say for sure if there was a sudden crisis or a build up of abnormally high extinction rates over centuries or millennia.

For this reason, the "mathematical artefacts" of extinction estimates were not sufficient to be certain about the current state of extinction, said MacLeod.

"If things aren't falling dead at your feel that doesn't mean you're not in the middle of a big extinction event," he said. "By the same token if the extinctions are and remain relatively modest then the changes, [even] aggregated over many years, are still going to end up a relatively modest extinction event."

Many Important Keystone and Predator Species Are at Risk

Douglas H. Chadwick

Douglas H. Chadwick is a wildlife biologist who conducts research on wolverines as a volunteer in Glacier National Park and serves as a founding board member of the conservation land trust Vital Ground. He also is the author of many books and magazine articles on natural history and conservation.

The day came clouded and wind-tossed, with 5 inches of fresh snow in the valley and a lot more piling up overhead on the peaks. It was early December in Montana in Glacier National Park. Although winter wouldn't officially start for another two weeks, blizzards and bitterly cold temperatures had long since sent the bears into their dens.

But not every bear.

Very large, very fresh paw prints on the trail in front of me said at least one grizzly wasn't ready to call it quits for the year.

Sleeping in underground dens keeps bears safe and insulated through the snow-smothered months while they live off reserves of fat. The biggest and most powerful ones—adult male grizzlies—sometimes leave their hidden chambers to roam about during midwinter thaws. Before, few naturalists realized these heavy-bodied bears could stay out through much colder conditions as long as they were able to take in more energy from food than they burned trying to find it. Then wolves returned to the American West.

The Food Web Surrounding Wolves

After an absence of half a century, wolves came back to Glacier during the 1980s, trotting across the border from neighboring Canadian wildlands. Suddenly, this Rocky Mountain landscape held more carcasses of deer, elk and moose, and those of us who frequented the slopes began to discover a few scavenging grizzlies later and later into the frozen season. One valley, with prime wintering grounds for hoofed herds, hosts a big male silvertip grizzly that I'm not sure ever holes up to snooze anymore.

Ecologists commonly depict the structure of natural communities as a pyramid.

Wolverines, with their unsurpassed nose for leftovers, can find more meals now as well. So can wintering bald eagles and golden eagles, along with northern ravens, which often follow wolf packs on the prowl. Wildlife biologists tracking the wolves discovered them taking over fresh kills made by mountain lions. In many cases, the packs seemed to be honing in on the sight of circling ravens or the birds' excited calls in order to find the stealthy cats and drive them off their prize. Before wolves were reintroduced to Yellowstone National Park in the mid-1990s, cougars had expanded their range to include broad valley bottoms. After the wolves' return, the cougars retreated to the steeper, more broken upland terrain they had normally hunted.

Animals ranging from jays and magpies to martens and black bears glean scraps from wolf-killed carcasses. Coyotes are on that list of opportunists as well, but the wolves are lethally intolerant of their closest kin. In fact, Yellowstone's new wolves quickly reduced the number of resident coyotes by nearly half, and forced survivors to take up life in smaller, more scattered territories. Coyotes behave much the same way toward their smaller relatives, suppressing the numbers and territories of foxes. So, where wolves move in, coyotes end up marginalized while foxes thrive. That in turn shifts the odds of survival for coyote prey such as hares and young deer, as well as for the small rodents and ground-nesting birds the foxes stalk. These changes affect how often certain roots, buds, seeds and insects get eaten, which can alter the balance of local plant communities, and so on down the food chain all the way to fungi and microbes.

Trophic Cascades: The Trickle-Down Effect

Ecologists commonly depict the structure of natural communities as a pyramid. The different layers are known as "trophic" (or feeding) levels. Green, solar-powered organisms—plants—form the foundation. On that broad base of primary producers rest layers of vegetarian species. Meat-eaters then stack up in smaller blocks above the herbivores until only the predators that have few or no predators themselves remain at the pyramid's peak.

Lately, wolves have actually declined in Yellowstone, partly because food is no longer as readily available.

Experts used to assume the overall richness of an ecosystem was determined by bottom-up influences—that is, by the fertility of the soil, climatic conditions such as annual precipitation, disruptions such as flooding or wildfire, and other environmental factors that bear upon plant growth. Only recently did researchers begin to notice how the addition or removal of a dominant predator—say, a jaguar or killer whale—reverberates through all the lower layers of the pyramid. This top-down effect is known as a "trophic cascade." Picture water spilling from a point source: The main flow fans out as it descends, splitting and splitting again, with a few streams jetting away to one side or another, then flowing on in more rivulets and arcs of spray.

Wolves are one such predator. This endangered species' natural recolonization of the Glacier Park area and subsequent reintroduction to Yellowstone sparked an array of close scientific studies, and the results are an ongoing revelation. At the start, the elk in Yellowstone were, in the view of many experts, overpopulated and degrading their range. Herds practically camped in areas such as brushy wetland meadows and riverside flood plains, concentrating on favorite foods such as willow, aspen and cottonwood. Over the years, those woody plants became pruned into misshapen bonsai forms by elk teeth. Finding a young one taller than shoulder height was rare. In quite a few places, the aspen stands were no longer reproducing at all. Some had already died out.

Predictably, after the wolves arrived, their population grew while elk numbers fell. Yet within a decade, the wolf and elk populations started to approach equilibrium. Lately, wolves have actually declined in Yellowstone, partly because food is no longer as readily available, partly from disease, and partly because wolves limit their own density within a given range through deadly fights over territories. From the standpoint of the ecosystem, the most important impact wolves had on Yellowstone elk was not simply readjusting the size of herds, but also causing them to spread out into different areas and keeping them on the move.

Relieved from the pressure of constant browsing, long stems shot up from the clubbed-looking shrubs and trees. New saplings arose from ground level. Groves thickened, attracting more songbirds and small mammals. The roots of recovering vegetation stabilized the shores of waterways. Lured by the flourishing woody plants, beavers moved in and raised families. Their dams further countered stream bank erosion, and at the same time created new pond and marsh habitats for moose, otters, mink, wading birds, waterfowl, fish, amphibians and more. Lush regrowth along the edges drew still more songbirds, and the burgeoning supply of insects fed nestlings. The insects dropped off overhanging leaves into the waterways, nourishing trout as well.

As these trends continue into the future, entire watersheds will become more productive and able to support a wider diversity of species. They'll also become more drought-resistant, with runoff water stored in beaver ponds and side channels able to help maintain streamflows through the hottest, driest months.

A trophic cascade doesn't always have to involve a top predator.

Glacier Park has denser, more varied forests where white-tailed deer abound, so the wolves there haven't been as tightly focused on elk. Just the same, the recovery of some heavily browsed sites has been as dramatic as in Yellowstone.

Long reviled as beasts of waste and desolation, wolves are looking more and more like creators of abundance and stability. Squint a bit, and you may even see generations of wolves in the keen senses and grace of elk, in the long-legged bulk and power of moose, in the electric reflexes of deer. Or, as poet Robinson Jeffers put it: "What but the wolf's tooth whittled so fine / The fleet limbs of the antelope?"

Surprising Keystone Species

A trophic cascade doesn't always have to involve a top predator. Back in the late 1960s, zoologist Robert Paine removed the starfish known as "ochre stars" from sample areas on the coast of Washington state. Active, aggressive hunters, ochre stars gorge on mussels. Lose that single predator, and thick beds of rapidly proliferating mussels take over, squeezing out barnacles, algae, snails, sponges, tube worms, sea squirts, and the rest of the remarkable mix of marine life usually at home in the intertidal zone. With ochre stars, Paine introduced the idea of a "keystone species," defining it as one that exerts an outsized effect within an ecosystem, not necessarily through sheer size, number or biomass, but because of the pivotal role it plays.

Sea otters aren't quite at the apex of the food chain along the North Pacific coast, for they can fall victim to sharks and killer whales. However, the otters dine on a smorgasbord of mollusks, crustaceans and, most of all, sea urchins. With the densest fur of any animal—650,000 hairs per square inch—they were once hunted to near extinction for their pelts. Not long afterward, people noticed kelp beds that had served as the otters' preferred habitat turning quite sparse or vanishing altogether. With the otters gone, it turned out, an exploding urchin population was gnawing its way through those submarine thickets of giant algae. Producing as much organic material per acre as tropical rain forests, kelp forests serve as sheltering nurseries for all kinds of juvenile fish, including commercially valuable species. Where kelp was most abundant, humans harvested it to make additives for products from soap and fertilizer to ice cream and jelly. Here, then, was a trophic cascade that tumbled down through unexpected levels and then washed onto us.

Vegans as Ecosystem Engineers

In another type of trophic cascade involving a keystone species, the lead role is played by a vegan: the African elephant. Consuming upward of 400 pounds of plants per day in the case of large males, these titans rip down tree limbs for meals, girdle tree trunks by stripping off nutritious bark, and simply push smaller trees over to get at the branches. As for shrubs, elephants not only eat the stems but tear whole plants to pieces, uproot others and trample still more underfoot while foraging.

When fully grown, elephants are virtually immune to predators, and herds tend to increase until checked by drought, food shortages or disease. At high population levels, their quest for food can transform wooded habitats into open plains. In cooperation with wildfire, elephants also maintain existing savannas by removing the woody plants that inevitably invade grasslands. Elephants shape the woodland-savanna balance in an ecosystem by determining the proportions of grazers such as gazelles, zebras and wildebeest to woody plant browsers such as giraffes and kudus, and of lions prowling the plains to leopards waiting to pounce from an overarching tree limb. That is, elephants shaped the communities in which our primate ancestors developed, stood upright and started walking toward the future.

The central fact [is] that everything in an ecosystem is connected to everything else.

Ecologists sometimes refer to elephants as "ecosystem architects" or "ecosystem engineers." Here in North America, grizzlies serve the same function. In addition to their effects as predators and scavengers of hoofed animals, the big bears fertilize streamside habitats with their waste and the remains of the salmon they eat. (Both are rich in nitrogen and other essential nutrients.) Grizzlies also distribute thousands of seeds from shrubs after eating the berries, and they rank as the chief animal earth-movers of the upper elevations in portions of the Rockies. Excavating acre upon acre to get at hibernating rodents and the bulbs and starchy roots of various herbs, they bring up nitrogen from deeper soil levels just as a farmer does when tilling fields. The seeds that fall into such freshly turned soil yield a more robust crop of new alpine and subalpine plants than seeds in undisturbed patches. Next time you're on a trail in grizzly range, instead of recalling some cheesy horror movie scene involving monster bruins, try thinking "heavyweight wildflower gardeners." It can't hurt.

Nature Is a Community

Everyone seems to have an opinion on ecology these days. Keep in mind, though, how new this field of science actually is, and how much all of us have yet to understand. Henry Ford had invented the automobile before biologist Ernst Haeckel even coined the term "ecology" early in the 20th century. The word didn't enter popular vocabulary until the 1960s.

Feeding-level pyramids, top predators, trophic cascades, keystone species, ecosystem engineers—these are all different expressions of the central fact that everything in an ecosystem is connected to everything else. A natural community is by no means just a collection of individual species. Its vitality comes from the relationships between those organisms—the interactions, the flow of energy and nutrients from each life to the next.

Comparatively rare to begin with, most of the world's apex carnivores are imperiled at present, and many keystone species are also at risk. There may be no more important lesson from the young science of ecology than this: If we want to keep ecosystems healthy and resilient, the first step is to pay closer attention to the way nature does this from the bottom up, and back down again from the top.

Climate Change Is Threatening Wild Animal Species Around the World

WWF

WWF, also called the World Wildlife Fund, is an environmental conservation organization that seeks to conserve priority places and species around the world.

Climate change and global warming impacts on species in a number of ways.

Animals and plants that are suited to cooler climates will need to move polewards or uphill when the climate becomes even just that little bit warmer.

This process has been observed in many places—in the Alps, in mountainous Queensland in Australia, and in the misty forests of Costa Rica.

Fish in the North Sea have been observed moving northwards too—fish stocks that used to be common around Cornwall have moved as far north as the Shetland and Orkney Islands.

The impacts on species are becoming so significant that their movements can be used as on indicator of a warming world. They are the silent witnesses of the rapid changes being inflicted on the Earth.

Species at Risk Around the World

Scientists predict that global warming could contribute to the mass extinction of wild animals in the near future.

An overheating world is creating a big change in climatic conditions and this can harm the delicate ecosystems in which species live. Threatened species can already be found all over the world—see the examples below.

The North Atlantic right whale is one of the most endangered of all large whales, with a long history of human exploitation.

Canada. The polar bear could disappear in the wild unless the pace of global warming slows. Dependent on sea ice, the animal uses it as a floating platform to catch prey. Experts believe that the Arctic sea ice is melting at a rate of 9% per decade, endangering the polar bear's habitat and existence.

South America. Sea turtles lay their eggs on Brazilian beaches, many of which are threatened by rising sea levels. Climate change also threatens the offspring of sea turtles, as nest temperature strongly determines the sex: the coldest sites produce male offspring, while the warmer sites produce female offspring.

This nest-warming trend is reducing the number of male offspring and seriously threatens turtle populations. . . .

America. The North Atlantic right whale is one of the most endangered of all large whales, with a long history of human exploitation. Since warming waters contain less plankton for whales to feed on, the availability of food due to climate fluctuations is also becoming an increasing cause of mortality. Between 300 and 350 individuals still exist, with little hope of population growth. . . .

China. The giant panda's future remains uncertain due to a number of threats. Its forest habitat in the mountainous areas of south-western China is fragmented, and giant panda populations are small and isolated from each other. Bamboo, the panda's staple diet, is also part of a delicate ecosystem that could be affected by the changes caused by global warming. Poaching too remains an everpresent threat, with only 1,600 individuals left in the wild. . . .

Indonesia. Asia's only ape—the orang-utan—is in deep trouble. Its last remaining strongholds in the rainforests of Indonesia are being threatened by a range of pressures, including climate change, putting the animal at risk of extinction within a few decades. With global warming increasing the duration and frequency of droughts, bushfires are occurring more often in these heavily logged forests, further fragmenting the orang-utan's living space. . . .

Africa. In Africa, elephants face a range of threats including shrinking living space, which brings them more frequently into conflict with people. With diminished living space, elephants will be unable to escape any changes to their natural habitat caused by global warming, including more frequent and longer dry periods, placing further pressure on their existence. . . .

Australia. Climate change is affecting home range, abundance and breeding cycles of many of Australia's frog species. Since frogs rely on water to breed, any reduction or change in rainfall could reduce frog reproduction. Higher temperatures contribute to the drying out of breeding pools, and as a result, to the deaths of tadpoles and eggs. Drier conditions also cause adult frogs to die, due to increased rates of internal water loss through their permeable skin.

India. Experts estimate there are as few as 3,200 tigers left in the wild, due to poaching, the loss of their habitat and depletion of the tiger's natural prey. Hunters, traders and poor local residents use the forest for subsistence, directly competing with the tiger. Some of the largest remaining areas where tigers occur are the mangrove forests of India. The projected rise in sea levels could cause these living spaces of the tiger to vanish altogether.

Climate Change and Other Human-Induced Impacts May Make a Mass Extinction of Ocean Species Inevitable

Environment News Service

Environment News Service is a daily international online wire service that provides late-breaking environmental news.

The oceans are at high risk of entering a phase of extinction of marine species unprecedented in human history, a panel of international marine experts warns in a report released today [June 21, 2011].

A deadly trio of factors—warming, acidification and lack of oxygen—is creating the conditions associated with every previous major extinction of species in Earth's history, the panel warned.

The combined effects of these stressors are causing degeneration in the ocean that is "far faster than anyone has predicted," the scientists report.

Shocking Findings

The urgent warnings emerged from the first-ever interdisciplinary international workshop held April 11–13 [2011] to consider the cumulative impact of all stressors affecting the ocean.

"The findings are shocking," said Dr. Alex Rogers, scientific director of the International Programme on the State of the Ocean which convened the workshop. "As we considered the cumulative effect of what humankind does to the ocean, the implications became far worse than we had individually realized."

"This is a very serious situation demanding unequivocal action at every level," warned Rogers, who specializes in the ecology, biodiversity and evolution of deep-sea ecosystems, with emphasis on cold-water corals, seamounts, hydrothermal vents and seeps.

> *[Marine scientists have] found firm evidence that the effects of climate change, coupled with other human-induced impacts . . . , have already caused a dramatic decline in ocean health.*

The first steps to globally significant extinction may have already begun with a rise in the extinction threat to marine species such as reef-forming corals, the scientists said, emphasizing that "the unprecedented speed of change" makes accurate assessment difficult.

"We are looking at consequences for humankind that will impact in our lifetime, and worse, our children's and generations beyond that," warned Rogers.

Leading Experts Agree

Marine scientists from institutions around the world gathered at Oxford University under the auspices of International Programme on the State of the Ocean and the International Union for the Conservation of Nature [IUCN]. The 27 participants from 18 organizations in six countries produced a grave assessment of current threats.

The group reviewed recent research by world ocean experts and found firm evidence that the effects of climate change, coupled with other human-induced impacts such as over-fishing and nutrient run-off from farming, have already caused a dramatic decline in ocean health.

Dan Laffoley, marine chair of IUCN's World Commission on Protected Areas and senior advisor on Marine Science and Conservation for IUCN, and co-author of the report, said,

"The world's leading experts on oceans are surprised by the rate and magnitude of changes we are seeing. The challenges for the future of the ocean are vast, but unlike previous generations we know what now needs to happen. The time to protect the blue heart of our planet is now, today and urgent."

Immediate Action Needed

The panel urges, "Immediate reduction in CO2 emissions coupled with significantly increased measures for mitigation of atmospheric CO2 and to better manage coastal and marine carbon sinks to avoid additional emissions of greenhouse gases. It is a matter of urgency that the ocean is considered as a priority in the deliberations of the IPCC [Intergovernmental Panel on Climate Change] and UNFCCC [United Nations Framework Convention on Climate Change]."

The panel members point out that the rate at which carbon is being absorbed by the ocean is already far greater now than at the time of the last globally significant extinction of marine species, some 55 million years ago, when up to 50 percent of some groups of deep sea animals were wiped out.

A single mass coral bleaching event in 1998 killed 16 percent of all the world's tropical coral reefs, they recalled, and overfishing has reduced some commercial fish stocks and populations of by-catch species by more than 90 percent.

New science indicates that pollutants such as flame retardants, fluorinated compounds and pharmaceuticals as well as synthetic musks found in detergents and personal care products have been located recently in the Canadian Arctic seas. Some are known to be endocrine disrupters or can damage immune systems.

These chemicals can be absorbed by tiny plastic particles in the ocean which are in turn ingested by marine creatures.

Meanwhile, continued releases and slow breakdown rates mean that legacy chemical pollution, such as from DDT, remains a major concern.

The marine experts agreed that adding these and other threats together means that the ocean and the ecosystems within it are unable to recover, being constantly bombarded with multiple attacks.

The report sets out a series of recommendations and calls on states, regional bodies and the United Nations to enact measures to better conserve ocean ecosystems, and in particular demands the urgent adoption of better governance of the largely unprotected high seas which make up the majority of the world's ocean.

Time available for action is shrinking, the panel warned. "The longer the delay in reducing emissions the higher the annual reduction rate will have to be and the greater the financial cost. Delays will mean increased environmental damage with greater socioeconomic impacts and costs of mitigation and adaptation measures."

Twenty Percent of Earth's Known Plant Species Are Threatened by Human Activities

Zachary Shahan

Zachary Shahan is a writer who specializes in environmental issues. He also is the editor or coeditor of three websites that focus on saving the environment: Cleantechnica.com, Planetsave.com, and Ecolocalizer.com.

We write about endangered species on here relatively often, but we generally focus on endangered animals. Of course, people relate more to animals than plants and are more touched by the thought of animal species disappearing forever than plant species disappearing forever, but I thought for this National Endangered Species Day [May 20, 2011] I'd give a little attention to the plants.

Plants are the basis of food chains. Plants are critical to all life on Earth and are a little underrated, I'd say. And there are a lot of them threatened with extinction.

The International Union for Conservation of Nature and Natural Resources (aka IUCN)—considered the most authoritative and comprehensive source for information on vulnerable, threatened, endangered, and critically endangered species—and the US Fish & Wildlife Service report a combined total of 9,322 endangered plant species. However, as I'll discuss below, this figure is probably a gross underestimate and a recent, monumental study finds the number to be over 80,000. With rapid destruction of unique ecosystems from human development, farming, and climate change, I think we can only expect the list of endangered plant species (combined with newly-extinct plant species) to grow in coming years.

Endangered Plants Underestimated

While 9,322 may look like a pretty high number, researchers have noted that this is sure to be tremendous underestimate of the true list of endangered plant species. The fact is, we don't have information on countless plant species, especially in tropical areas of the world where most plants live and where there is tremendous habit destruction.

A September 2010 study conducted by the Royal Botanic Gardens found that 22% of the approximately 380,000 known plant species (or about 83,600 plant species) are endangered. That's approximately 9 times what the IUCN and US Fish & Wildlife currently have listed.

The United States was once considered the world leader in endangered plant species.

"This study confirms what we already suspected, that plants are under threat and the main cause is human induced habitat loss," the Royal Botanic Gardens Kew's Director, Professor Stephen Hopper, says.

"We cannot sit back and watch plant species disappear—plants are the basis of all life on earth, providing clean air, water, food and fuel. All animal and bird life depends on them and so do we. Having the tools and knowledge to turn around loss of biodiversity is now more important than ever and the Sampled Red List Index for Plants gives conservationists and scientists one such tool."

According to this updated study, based on species percentages, plants are "more threatened than birds, as threatened as mammals and less threatened than amphibians or corals."

U.S. a World Leader in Endangered Plants?

The United States was once considered the world leader in endangered plant species. Though, this was mostly due to better research and scientific understanding of the issues in the United States. (However, it should be noted that the U.S. has an even higher rate of forest loss than Indonesia and Brazil and it is definitely still a problem in the U.S.)

The Royal Botanic Gardens report, though, . . . now shows South America, South Africa, Mexico, China, Australia, and Indonesia as the areas where plants are the most threatened.

Tropical rain forests are where plants are most threatened, the report found, due to habit loss that mostly results from "conversion of natural habitats for agriculture or livestock use." . . .

What You Can Do to Prevent Plant Extinctions

There are a handful of things you can clearly do to prevent plant extinctions (and prevent more plants from ending up on this humongous list), many of which we emphasize . . . every chance we get:

1. Grow your own food as much as possible, buy local as much as possible, and eat vegetarian to cut down on deforestation;

2. Help prevent global warming from escalating by greening your transport, greening your diet, and cutting the coal;

3. Urge leading supermarkets and restaurants to not buy products related to deforestation or habitat destruction (and don't buy products related to such things);

4. Urge your representatives in government to fight global warming.

Really, that is what is most needed.

List of Officially Endangered Plants

If you want to see a comprehensive list of officially endangered plants, Earth's Endangered Creatures provides one that is continually updated, based on data from the US Fish & Wildlife List of Endangered Species and the IUCN Red List of Endangered Species (the total number at the time of writing this, as mentioned above, is 9,322 and is actually a tremendous underestimate of the actual list).

The Spread of High-Yield Crops Is Depleting Agricultural Biodiversity

Fahim Nawaz

Fahim Nawaz is a writer who contributes to Dawn.com, an on-line media source that provides breaking news, current events, and top stories from Pakistan, South Asia, and elsewhere in the world.

The replacement of indigenous varieties of crops, fruits, vegetables and livestock species by high-yield crop varieties and improved breeds of animals, in the past few decades, has depleted agro-biodiversity.

The Loss of Agro-Biodiversity

Indigenous varieties and livestock species have lost their significance due to intensification of farming and separation of local communities from indigenous biological resources.

Agro-biodiversity has a major role in providing food and promoting food security for the future. Agro-biodiversity for food and agriculture comprises various biological diversity components like crops, fish, livestock, pests, inter-acting species of pollinators, predators and competitors among others. About 20,000 species of plants, fungi and animals have been identified for their medicinal importance; and pharmaceutical industry is based on these biological resources and related local knowledge. Plants are the potential food resource for both humans and animals. It is interesting to know that about 30,000 plants species have edible parts but only 7,000 plants have been collected or grown as food throughout the history, of which only 20 species provide 90 per cent of the world's food. Wheat, rice and maize supply 60 per cent of the world food requirements.

Livestock is so severely affected that about 30 per cent of its breeds are at risk of extinction and six breed[s], worldwide, are lost each month.

The food security is threatened by rapid decline of biodiversity through introduction of exotic species, loss of gene pool, neglected/underutilised species, monocultures and biofuels. The introduction of uniform, high-yielding varieties has resulted in the loss of 75 per cent of plant genetic diversity as farmers have worldwide replaced their multiple local varieties and landraces with these varieties. These varieties led to the deterioration of the environment as they required more water, high input of chemical fertilisers and pesticides which increased salinity, waterlogging and also resulted in depletion of nutrients.

The well adapted old cultivars have been replaced by few genetically modified varieties and breeds. New species are ranked second to habitat destruction in threatening the biodiversity as they exclude native species by competing with native flora/fauna for resources. Some plants like Mesquite have made cultivated lands vulnerable to cultivation while others like eucalyptus and parthenium retard seed germination and plant growth of native plants by releasing allelopathic chemicals. It has also resulted in the introduction of new pests like mealy bug.

Livestock is so severely affected that about 30 per cent of its breeds are at risk of extinction and six breed[s], worldwide, are lost each month. Domestic animals are decreasing at the rate of five per cent and tropical forests at the rate of one per cent. About 70 per cent of marine species are fully exploited and nearly 60 per cent of the earth's coral reefs are threatened by humans. According to estimates 34,000 species of plants or 12.5 per cent of the world's flora are facing extinction. The diminishing biological resources will diminish food sources of the communities and this will lead to food insecurity.

The introduction of bio-fuels in the last few decades has helped solve the problem of energy insecurity and climate change but the increased conversion of agricultural commodities to biofuels resulted in an increase of international food prices.

According to the World Bank, about 70–75 per cent of the increase in food commodity prices from 2002 to 2008 was mainly due to biofuels. The use of biofuels has decisively contributed to a rising demand for sugar, maize, wheat, oilseeds, and palm oil and this food/fuel competition could be observed as global wheat and maize stocks are declining considerably.

Agriculture intensification has reduced crop diversity to few varieties in Gilgit-Baltistan region of Pakistan. Buck wheat was grown on wide scale earlier but now it is rarely seen in the fields of the region because farmers are keen to grow potatoes and high-yielding wheat varieties which have made their fields susceptible to pests and diseases. The infestation of the pests like codling moth and wooly aphids in apples, Botrytis leaf virus in onions, crown gall disease in cherries and nematodes in potatoes are the effects of agriculture intensification. The market oriented agriculture practices, during the last few decades in the region, have replaced traditional self-sustaining agriculture systems.

Government Intervention Needed

Support to farmers is required as they play a key role in the protection of precious resources. It should be provided as a means of meeting the survival needs of ever increasing population. They should be given subsidy to encourage them to grow old, neglected and underutilised crop species like pearl millet, finger millet and sorghum etc. Biopiracy and patents on living organisms should be prohibited as well as the prohibition of the development of sterile varieties through genetic engineering processes. The government should redesign policies and take serious efforts for the conservation of biodiversity in the country. The establishment of gene bank at regional levels and promotion of research related to evaluation of national germplasm would help in this regard.

CHAPTER 3

Are Human Food Production Methods a Threat to Earth's Biodiversity?

Chapter Preface

The fastest growing type of agriculture is aquaculture—the farming of fish and aquatic plants in either fresh or salt water environments. Although capture fisheries—that is, catching wild fish—is still the main method used by commercial fish producers, aquaculture already accounts for 25 percent of world fish production and is expected to increase significantly in the future. Many types of finfish, crustaceans, and mollusks are grown this way, but the most common are finfish species—such as carp, tilapia, catfish, and trout. Other cultivated species include oysters, shrimp, and salmon, along with plants such as kelp and seaweed. Aquaculture production systems use inland ponds, lakes, or tanks and cages or pens in coastal or ocean areas. The global demand for fish is rising along with the human population, and aquaculture helps to relieve pressure on overexploited and declining wild fish populations; but increasingly scientists and critics argue that its overall impact on the environment and biodiversity is extremely negative.

One concern is that fish in aquaculture pens—which may be non-native to the area and/or genetically engineered—can escape their enclosures, affecting wild fish and their ecosystems. This fear is not speculative; there have been many instances of fish escapes. In some cases, escaping fish can act as predators, posing a threat to native fish species. For example, some critics claim that the introduction of striped bass from the Atlantic coast of the United States to the Pacific coast has reduced the populations of Chinook salmon in the Sacramento–San Joaquin Delta region. Cultured fish that invade local fish habitats can also compete with resident fish species for food and other resources. Many environmentalists fear that aquaculture-grown Atlantic salmon, which has been genetically altered to grow at twice the rate of wild salmon, will out-compete wild salmon or contaminate the native gene pools, eventually replacing wild species.

The spread of disease is another serious concern associated with aquaculture farming. As new non-native fish species are introduced to water ecosystems, they can bring with them parasites and disease pathogens that wreak havoc in these new environments. Local fish often have no resistance to these new threats and can be decimated in a short time. The import of Atlantic salmon from Sweden or Norway, for example, is believed by experts to have introduced a new parasite to local wild salmon populations in the 1970s. In some cases, the disease might be more virulent in the new environment. Taiwan's shrimp industry collapsed in the early 1990s, reportedly because shrimp carrying new viruses were introduced, causing losses of more than a billion dollars. The introduction of exotic fish species can also cause a cascade of effects throughout the local ecosystem and in some cases change aquatic habitats by displacing other fish species and plant material, reducing biodiversity.

In addition, like any type of intensive farming, aquaculture uses chemicals and produces wastes that can cause environmental pollution. One type of pollution is eutrophication—the contamination of waters by fish fecal wastes and excess fish food. Eutrophication increases the nutrient levels of the water, encouraging the growth of algae which, in turn, decompose and deplete the oxygen in the water. Without oxygen, many fish and marine organisms cannot live, so this type of pollution poses a high risk to marine environments. Moreover, some species of phytoplantkton actually benefit from the higher levels of nutrients, and some of these are toxic to other marine organisms and to humans. An example of this is red tides, which produce toxins that can be ingested by mussels and oysters, creating a health risk for people who consume them. Another type of aquaculture pollution comes from the use of antibiotics and other chemicals used to keep cultured fish healthy and keep cages and nets clean.

Aquaculture has other environmental impacts, too. Many aquaculture fisheries rely on wild fish for fish food. Although aquafeed is typically made from bycatch—so-called trash fish caught unintentionally along with targeted fish—or from species such as mackerel that are not usually consumed by humans, this practice helps to deplete natural fish stocks at a time when they are already threatened by overfishing. Also, some aquaculture operations have been located in ecologically sensitive areas, completely destroying the natural environment. A good example is in Asia, where hundreds of thousands of acres of mangrove forests—trees that grow in coastal saline waters in the tropics and subtropics—have been converted to shrimp farms and destroyed in the process. Mangrove forests, similar to salt marshes, play a critical environmental role by preventing soil and beach erosion, maintaining water quality, and providing habitat and nurseries for many marine creatures. Perhaps the worst part is that shrimp farms typically are subject to disease, so they often are productive only temporarily; yet once the aquaculture is gone, it is very difficult to restore mangroves. The environmental cost, therefore, is huge.

Aquaculture proponents claim that aquaculture farms, if properly managed and regulated, can protect the environment and at the same time fulfill the much-needed role of feeding the world's growing human population. Many countries are beginning to closely monitor and regulate aquaculture facilities. However, developing countries often fail to create or enforce these legal controls to ensure sustainable fish operations. Whether fish farms are regulated or not, most observers expect aquaculture to continue its pattern of growth due to the great demand for fish products. The authors of the viewpoints in this chapter address the question of whether other types of agriculture pose a major threat to Earth's biodiversity.

Industrial Agriculture Is a Major Threat to Biodiversity

Sustainable Table

Sustainable Table is a website created in 2003 by the nonprofit organization GRACE to help consumers understand the problems with the human food supply and offer viable solutions.

Short for biological diversity, biodiversity is the variety of all life in a given area—this area could be as small as your backyard, or as large as the entire planet.[i] Biodiversity includes not only the variety of species of plants and animals (species diversity), but also the variety of genes contained in all individual organisms (genetic diversity), and the variety of habitats, biological communities, and ecological processes (ecosystem diversity).[ii]

Biodiversity is essential for our existence because the earth's biological systems and processes provide us with food, materials for clothing and shelter, fuel, medicine, clean water, and clean air. Biodiversity also provides all other species with the resources required for their survival. In fact, given the interdependence of the Earth's living organisms, ecosystems, and biological processes, without biodiversity, life on Earth would become extinct.

Unfortunately, the Earth is currently experiencing a rapid loss of biodiversity. Human-induced environmental destruction has eliminated habitats, killed living organisms, reduced genetic diversity, and caused the rate of species extinction to increase dramatically. In fact, unsustainable human activity is now the greatest threat to biodiversity.

Biodiversity and Agriculture

Humans are directly dependent upon a variety of plants and animals that provide our supply of food. Furthermore, the production of these foodstuffs involves a variety of ecological processes and the activities of many different living organisms. Without biodiversity, none of our food could be produced.

According to the United Nations Food and Agriculture Organization (FAO), we are currently losing an average of 2 domestic animal breeds each week.

Here are a few essential agricultural processes made possible by Earth's biodiversity:

• Pest Control

• Natural predators such as wasps and birds help reduce populations of pests that destroy plants on farms.

• Pollination

• Many of the world's staple crops are pollinated by insects, birds, bats and other animals.

• Productive Soil

• A variety of living organisms take part in the decomposition processes that create soils and make nutrients available for plants to use.

• Resistance to Disease and Pests

• Genetic diversity helps to provide resistance to disease and pests—mass production of a single crop variety makes it easier for a disease or pest to wipe-out the entire crop.

Unfortunately, industrial agriculture has caused a dramatic reduction of genetic diversity within the animal and plant species typically used for food. About 7,000 different species of plants have been raised as food crops in the history of human agriculture. Yet in part because of modern tendencies towards mass production, only fifteen plant and eight animal species are now relied upon for about 90% of all human food.[iii] As a result of this homogenization of the food industry, thousands of noncommercial animal breeds and crop varieties have disappeared, along with the valuable genetic diversity they possessed.

Farm Animals

Centuries of natural and human selection have created thousands of breeds within each of the major domesticated animal species. Since each breed has slightly different genetic traits, different breeds are better suited for different environmental conditions. For instance, certain breeds are adapted to withstand extreme heat; others are adapted to withstand extreme cold, others are especially resistant to disease, while others are adapted to survive periods of drought, etc.

While none of the major species of domesticated livestock or poultry are in danger of extinction, other livestock breeds are disappearing rapidly. According to the United Nations Food and Agriculture Organization (FAO), we are currently losing an average of 2 domestic animal breeds each week,[iv] and half of all domestic animal breeds that existed in Europe in 1900 are now extinct.[v] In the past fifteen years alone, the FAO has identified the extinction of 300 out of 6000 breeds worldwide, with another 1,350 in danger of extinction.[vi]

The decline in livestock diversity has resulted largely from the rise of industrial agriculture. Factory farms mass-produce only a few select livestock breeds that have been specially chosen to maximize production of meat, milk, or eggs. Since industrial agriculture's domination of the meat and dairy industries continues to force independent farmers out of business, the heritage livestock breeds raised by these farmers are quickly disappearing. This has caused a sharp decrease in the genetic diversity of the world's livestock populations.

The loss of genetic diversity in livestock poses several significant problems. First, industrial production has created a system in which livestock breeds are no longer suited to local environmental conditions. Instead, industrial livestock breeds have been bred to live in a carefully-regulated environment. In order to survive, these animals require costly inputs such as climate-controlled housing, regular doses of antibiotics, and large quantities of high-protein feed.[viii] Unlike hearty, traditional breeds which are adapted to withstand harsh environmental conditions, industrial livestock breeds are often unable to survive outside of the factory farm.

Since 1900, approximately 75% of the world's genetic diversity of agricultural crops has been eliminated.

It is crucial that diverse livestock breeds be preserved, as they serve as an important genetic resource. When a breed goes extinct, its unique genes are lost forever and can't be used to give new traits to existing livestock breeds. Unlike industrial farms that promote a few, limited breeds and a narrow gene pool, sustainable farms help to preserve valuable traits within livestock breeds so that future breeds can endure harsh conditions and survive outbreaks of disease.[ix]

Crops

Industrial farms currently mass-produce only a few genetic varieties of each crop used for food. These commercial crop varieties are specially bred for uniform appearance, disease-resistance, and for their ability to endure lengthy transport. Unfortunately, when farmers abandon traditional varieties to begin planting mass-produced commercial varieties, the traditional varieties can quickly become extinct.

Each plant variety contains unique genetic information that tells it how to grow. While all the varieties of a given species have many similar traits, each variety has a different genetic composition and therefore slightly different characteristics. The genetic composition of a fruit or vegetable variety not only influences its appearance and flavor, but also affects characteristics such as the plant's ability to withstand extreme temperatures and resist pests and diseases.

When non-commercial plant varieties become extinct, we not only lose the distinctive flavors and appearances of these fruits, vegetables and grains, we also lose the genetic diversity that they otherwise contribute to the plant stock. According to the Food and Agriculture Organization of the United Nations, since 1900, approximately 75% of the world's genetic diversity of agricultural crops has been eliminated.[xiii]

Industrial agriculture also reduces biodiversity by damaging the natural environment through pollution from untreated animal waste, chemicals and soil erosion.

As the number of crop varieties decrease (reducing the genetic diversity of these plant species), existing crops become increasingly susceptible to devastation by disease and pests. If crops are all the same, it's much easier for a new disease or pest to wipe-out an entire harvest. Indeed, the lack of genetic diversity has contributed to widespread crop-loss in the past— for example:

- In 1970, US farmers lost $1 billion worth of crops after a disease killed uniform corn varieties.[xiv]

- Lack of genetic diversity led to massive outbreaks of citrus canker in Florida in 1984 and in Brazil in 1991.[xv]

- During the 1840's, the majority of the population of Ireland relied upon a single variety of the potato. As a result of the lack of genetic diversity, a fungus was able to destroy the entire potato crop, causing the infamous Irish Potato Famine.[xvi]

The rapid reduction of genetic diversity also makes it more difficult for plant breeders to develop new crop varieties. In order to protect plants from newly emerging diseases and pests, commercial plant breeders use traditional, non-industrial plant varieties to breed resistance into the existing commercial crop varieties. However, the rapid disappearance of non-industrial plant varieties is quickly eliminating this source of genetic material, thus compromising our ability to adapt crops to suit changing conditions. This jeopardizes the future security of our food supply.

Environmental Damage

Industrial agriculture also reduces biodiversity by damaging the natural environment through pollution from untreated animal waste, chemicals and soil erosion. Excessive amounts of manure created by the thousands of animals found on large industrial farms create air, groundwater and surface water pollution. In addition, industrial agriculture uses enormous amounts of pesticides and chemical fertilizers that leach into the ground and water, polluting the surrounding environment. Factory farms generate tremendous amounts of pollution. While concentrated animal feeding operations (CAFOs) contaminate soil, water and air with vast quantities of untreated manure, industrial crop producers pollute the environment with enormous amounts of chemical pesticides and fertilizers. These pollutants kill living organisms and destroy the natural environment. Since the loss of genetic diversity makes plants increasingly vulnerable to devastation by pests, industrial farms compensate by using increased amounts of chemical pesticides. Unfortunately, these substances cause significant damage to local and regional ecosystems. Extensive pesticide use is particularly harmful to insect populations, including those that are important to the environment. The US honey-bee population—responsible for pollinating an estimated 15–30% of all food consumed in the United States—has been reduced by about half in the past fifty years by the toxic chemicals present in pesticides.[xvii]

Pollution caused by excessive use of chemical fertilizers and over-application of manure degrades waterways and kills aquatic organisms by depleting the oxygen content of the water. Heavy use of nitrogen fertilizers on industrial farms can also reduce biodiversity because only certain plants will grow well in nitrogen-rich environments, and these plants will crowd out other species.[xx]

What You Can Do

A growing number of sustainable farmers are preserving agricultural variety and protecting biodiversity by raising "heritage" and "heirloom" animal breeds, fruits, and vegetables. As responsible stewards of the land, sustainable farmers raise only as many animals as the land is capable of handling, and avoid using harmful pesticides and chemical fertilizers. By supporting these farmers, you can help promote biodiversity and protect valuable breeds of animals and plants from facing extinction. Visit the Eat Well Guide [an online database] to find a farm, market or restaurant near you that sells meat, eggs and dairy products from heritage animals, and visit a local farmers market to find heirloom fruits and vegetables. Also, buy organic foods—these foods were not grown with chemical fertilizers or the pesticides that deplete biodiversity.

Sources

1. Rediscovering Biology. "Biodiversity." Annenberg/CPB 2004.
2. Ibid.
3. United Nations Convention of Biological Diversity. *Agricultural Biodiversity: Introduction.* 2005 (accessed October 12, 2006).

4. Food and Agriculture Organization. "Biological Diversity in Food and Agriculture: Domestic Animal Genetic Diversity." FAO (accessed October 12, 2006).
5. Food and Agriculture Organization of the United Nations. "Special: Biodiversity for Food and Agriculture: Farm Animal Genetic Resources." FAO. February 1998.
6. Food and Agriculture Organization. "Biological Diversity in Food and Agriculture: Domestic Animal Genetic Diversity." FAO (accessed October 12, 2006).
7. Food and Agriculture Organization of the United Nations. "Special: Biodiversity for Food and Agriculture: Farm Animal Genetic Resources." FAO. February 1998.
8. Food and Agriculture Organization of the United Nations. "Special: Biodiversity for Food and Agriculture: Farm Animal Genetic Resources." FAO. February 1998.
9. University of Missouri. "American Livestock Breed Conservancy." *Ag Opportunities*. August 21, 1998.
10. Food and Agriculture Organization of the United Nations. "Special: Biodiversity for Food and Agriculture: Farm Animal Genetic Resources." FAO. February 1998.
11. Rural Advancement Foundation International (RAFI). The Seed Giants—Who Owns Whom? RAFI. 2000.
12. Fernandez-Cornejo, Jorge, and David Schimmelpfennig. "Have Seed Industry Changes Affected Research Effort?," Amber Waves 2:1 (February 2004): 18.
13. Food and Agriculture Organization of the United Nations. "Special: Biodiversity for Food and Agriculture: Crop Genetic Resources." FAO. February 1998.
14. World Resources Institute, IUCN—The World Conservation Union, United Nations Environment Program (UNEP). Chapter 2, "Losses of Biodiversity and Their Causes," in Global Biodiversity Strategy: Guidelines for action to save, study and use Earth's biotic wealth sustainably and equitably. World Resources Institute. 1992.
15. Ibid.

16. Ibid.
17. Roach, John. "Bee Decline May Spell End of Some Fruits, Vegetables." *National Geographic News*. 5 October 2004 (accessed October 12, 2006).
18. Ribaudo, Marc, and Robert Johansson. "Water Quality Impacts of Agriculture," in *Agricultural Resources and Environmental Indicators*, 2006 Edition. USDA Economic Research Service, Economic Information Bulletin 16, July 2006: 36.
19. Roach, John. "Gulf of Mexico 'Dead Zone' Is Size of New Jersey." *National Geographic News*. 25 May 2005 (accessed 20 September 2006).
20. Horrigan, Leo, Robert S. Lawrence, and Polly Walker. "How Sustainable Agriculture Can Address the Environmental and Human Health Harms of Industrial Agriculture." *Environmental Health Perspectives*, Vol 110, 5 May 2002.

Concentrated Animal Agriculture Is the Biggest Threat to the Environment and Biodiversity

Humane Society International

Humane Society International is an international animal protection organization that works to protect all animals, including animals in laboratories, farm animals, companion animals, and wildlife.

The intensification of farm animal production in industrialized agricultural systems, or factory farms, compromises animal welfare and degrades the environment. Animal agriculture inefficiently consumes natural resources, contributes to deforestation, and produces immense quantities of animal waste, threatening water and air quality and contributing to climate change. The Food and Agriculture Organization (FAO) of the United Nations estimated in 2006 that animal agriculture was responsible for 18% of global, anthropogenic, or human-induced, greenhouse gas emissions and was "by far the single largest anthropogenic user of land."

Factory Farming in Brazil

Over 67 billion land animals were raised globally for human consumption in 2008, and global meat and milk production are projected to approximately double between 1999 and 2050. Brazil is the world's largest meat exporter and 2009 statistics show that its cattle herd is the largest in the world at over 200 million animals. Per capita meat consumption nearly doubled in Brazil between 1980 and 2005, and Brazilian beef production and exports were expected to rise by 3% in 2010 compared to 2009.

Geographical concentration of farm animal production can cause significant air and water pollution.

Farm animal operations are industrializing in developing nations, with rapidly increasing demand for meat and milk driving this industry transformation. Unlike pasture-based or mixed farming systems, today's concentrated farm animal production facilities, or factory farms, often confine tens of thousands of animals in factory-like facilities. These operations are becoming more widespread throughout the world, and can bring along devastating environmental consequences. According to the FAO, industrial systems now produce approximately two-thirds of the world's poultry meat and eggs, and more than half of all pork. In fact, "[i]n recent years industrial livestock production has grown at twice the rate of more traditional mixed farming systems and at more than six times the rate of production based on grazing."

At the same time, there is increasing standardization and consolidation of production in developing countries through vertical integration, in which the retailer contracts with suppliers and/or processors, as well as full integration, in which all units in the food chain are owned by one company. This evolution includes the animal agriculture sector and is present in Latin America, where there is a trend towards vertical integration. For example, 40% of Brazil's market for broiler chickens is supplied by just four integrators. In Brazil's dairy industry, the number of milk producers fell by approximately 23% between 2000 and 2002, while maintaining the same volume of milk production. This consolidation may have deleterious effects on rural farmers, as it often "eliminates open market competition and drives down prices paid to growers." Small farmers that try to directly compete with large animal agribusiness are at risk of being pushed out of the market because they lack the political and economic power of the larger companies, or the ability to exploit economies of scale.

Not only is farm animal production becoming consolidated in developing countries, the facilities themselves are becoming more geographically clustered. In Brazil, these high levels of geographical concentration can be seen in the pork and poultry industries. For example, in 1992, 78% of Brazil's hen population resided in only 5% of the country's area: in 2001, this number grew to 85%, while occupying the same total land area. Over the same time period, Brazil's pig population rose from 45% to 56% on only 5% of the country's area. This geographical concentration of farm animal production can cause significant air and water pollution.

The Environmental Threat of Animal Agriculture

In 2006, the FAO published "Livestock's Long Shadow: Environmental Issues and Options," its landmark report assessing the impacts of animal agriculture. The FAO concluded that "the livestock sector emerges as one of the top two or three most significant contributors to the most serious environmental problems, at every scale from local to global." With global meat and milk production expected to approximately double within the next 50 years, the FAO cautions that the "environmental impact per unit of livestock production must be cut by half, just to avoid increasing the level of damage beyond its present level." . . .

Farm Animal Waste. Much of the environmental damage caused by factory farms, in which each farm may confine up to hundreds of thousands of animals, is due to the volume and content of animal waste, and the consequent challenges of storage and disposal. In fact, "[o]ne animal facility with a large population of animals can easily equal a small city in terms of waste production."

Mixed farming systems connect the animal agriculture activity to the crops. On these systems farmers balance the number of animals with the land's ability to absorb the nutrients in their manure. Factory farms confine large numbers of animals on a disproportionately small land area, breaking this link between crop production and animal husbandry. In particularly high production areas, this has resulted in factory farms producing more manure than can be assimilated by available land, causing environmental damage.

Deforestation causes approximately 17% of the world's human-induced GHG emissions, by releasing stored carbon into the atmosphere.

Factory farm animal waste, which is stored in lagoons or pits, contains chemical contaminants as well as numerous pathogens. Potentially contaminating water, soil, and air, factory farms typically spray minimally treated or untreated waste on fields. Manure storage lagoons can also overflow. Pathogens from the manure may end up in surface water, and nutrients such as nitrogen and phosphorous can leach into groundwater and run off of fields. Waste storage and application also emit carbon dioxide, hydrogen sulfide, ammonia, methane, and particulates into the atmosphere. Nitrogen can also volatilize into ammonia emissions that are then redeposited into waterways. In fact, according to the FAO, "[t]he livestock sector . . . is probably the largest sectoral source of water pollution, contributing to eutrophication, 'dead' zones in coastal areas, degradation of coral reefs, human health problems, emergence of antibiotic resistance and many others."

In part to promote growth, farm animals are given large amounts of antibiotics and other drugs, and consequently, produce manure that includes these drug residues. Because the animal's digestion does not degrade all of the drugs, antibiotic and other drug residues are excreted into the environment and have been found to contaminate ground, surface, and tap water. According to the World Health Organization, "[a] growing body of evidence establishes a link between the use of antimicrobials in food-producing animals and the emergence of resistance among common pathogens."

In addition to antibiotics and other drugs, heavy metals are added to animal feed. Animals are capable of absorbing only 5 to 15% of these toxic metals, and increased feed conversion efficiency results in manure and slurry with an even higher concentration of metals than the enriched feed. Applying factory farm manure degrades the environment because the metals can accumulate in the soil, and potentially poison plants and animals.

Deforestation contributes to environmental degradation, including loss of biodiversity, soil degradation, and water pollution.

Deforestation. Nearly one-third (31%) of the earth's land is covered by forests, which act as net carbon sinks, releasing less carbon than they store. In fact, the world's forests retain about 289 billion tonnes of carbon. Deforestation causes approximately 17% of the world's human-induced GHG emissions, by releasing stored carbon into the atmosphere.

Pasture expansion for livestock is a key driver of deforestation, especially in Latin America, and it is estimated that "some 70 percent of previously forested land in the Amazon is used as pasture, and feed crops cover a large part of the remainder." Since the 1970s, Brazil, in particular, has suffered extensive deforestation in its Amazon region for cattle ranching. The FAO estimates that 16.9 million hectares of the Legal Amazon were deforested from 2000 through 2008. Between 1990 and 2002, Brazil's cattle population located in the Amazon expanded from approximately 18% to 31%, which represents 80% of Brazil's total cattle herd growth during this period. A World Bank paper found that in 2004 "[c]attle ranching enterprises . . . [occupied] nearly 75 percent of the deforested areas of Amazonia." With this in mind, it is no surprise that cattle ranching is the main contributor to deforestation in the Brazilian Amazon.

Soybean production for animal feed is another emerging cause of rainforest destruction. According to a 2006 FAO report, the cultivation of soybean and corn for animal feed contributes to the clearing of forests in Brazil and Latin America. Over 97% of global soymeal production is fed to animals used in agriculture, and during the last four decades of the 20th century, over 60% of the corn and barley crop were also fed to these animals. Globally, soybean production increased rapidly in recent decades, and expanding production is currently due to demand for animal feed. A 2010 study of Amazonian deforestation during the years 2000–2006 concluded that "even if the proximate cause of deforestation was mainly ranching, it is likely that soy cultivation is a major *underlying* cause."

Deforestation contributes to environmental degradation, including loss of biodiversity, soil degradation, and water pollution. In Brazil, Amazon deforestation emits more CO_2 than any other source.

Enteric fermentation, which is microbial fermentation that takes place in the digestive systems of ruminant animals . . . , accounted for 63.2% of Brazil's methane emissions in 2005.

Greenhouse Gas Emissions (GHGs) and Climate Change. The FAO estimated in 2006 that animal agriculture is responsible for 18% of global, anthropogenic GHGs. The animal agriculture sector is one of the most important sectors for policies aimed at immediate and swift reductions in humans' climate impacts.

Essentially every part of the animal production chain pollutes the air or contributes to climate change. The sector emits significant amounts of three of the most important GHGs: carbon dioxide (CO_2), methane (CH_4), and nitrous oxide (N_2O). In fact, globally the farm animal sector accounts for:

- 9% of human-induced CO_2 emissions

- 35–40% of human-induced CH_4 emissions, which has 25 times the global warming potential (GWP), or power, of CO_2 over 100 years, and

- 65% of human-induced N_2O emissions, which has about 300 times the GWP of CO_2.

CO_2: Carbon dioxide emissions from this sector are produced through nitrogen fertilizer production for feed, on-farm fossil fuel use, deforestation to make way for grazing and animal feed production (~2.4 billion tonnes), and pasture desertification, which can result from overgrazing by farm animals. An estimated 41 million tonnes of CO_2 are emitted from fertilizer production for feed crops each year. Brazil, alone, emits 1.69 million tonnes of CO_2 per year from fossil fuel use in the production of nitrogen fertilizer for feed.

CH_4: Enteric fermentation and manure management are the key causes of animal agriculture's methane emissions. Enteric fermentation, which is microbial fermentation that takes place in the digestive systems of ruminant animals, such as cattle, sheep, and buffalo, accounted for 63.2% of Brazil's methane emissions in 2005. Globally, this process accounts for 25% of animal agriculture's total GHG emissions. Manure is responsible for the remaining portion of methane emissions from farm animals and accounts for approximately 5% of animal agriculture's GHG emissions.

N_2O: The farm animal sector also is responsible for the majority of the world's human-induced nitrous oxide emissions. Nitrous oxide emissions from animal agriculture originate primarily from manure and fertilizer for feed crops, and contribute approximately 31% of animal agriculture's GHG emissions.

Mitigation Actions Essential

Mitigating the animal agriculture sector's significant yet underappreciated role in climate change and environmental problems is vital for the health and sustainability of the planet, and its human and nonhuman inhabitants. As "the single largest anthropogenic user of land" and responsible for an estimated 18% of human-induced GHG emissions, the farm animal production sector must be held accountable for its many deleterious impacts, and changes in animal agricultural practices must be achieved. Individually, incorporating environmentally sound and animal welfare-friendly practices into daily life, including a reduction in meat, milk, and egg consumption, can reduce our environmental impact.

Humane Society International (HSI) calls for critical actions each of us can and should take:

- Reduce: A shift towards plant-based foods can achieve GHG reductions. By making flexitarian, vegetarian, and vegan lifestyle choices, each of us can reduce our environmental impact.

- Refine: Refining the diet by switching to higher-welfare animal products helps diminish animal suffering and protect the environment.

- Replace: The consequences of replacing animal products with healthy vegetarian options are enormous—not only for farm animals, but for public health and environmental integrity as well.

Slash and Burn Agriculture Results in Tropical Habitat and Biodiversity Loss

Colin Stief

Colin Stief is a geographer who worked as an intern in the fall of 2008 for About.com, a website owned by The New York Times *that provides original information and advice.*

Slash and burn agriculture is the process of cutting down the vegetation in a particular plot of land, setting fire to the remaining foliage, and using the ashes to provide nutrients to the soil for use of planting food crops.

The cleared area following slash and burn, also known as swidden, is used for a relatively short period of time, and then left alone for a longer period of time so that vegetation can grow again. For this reason, this type of agriculture is also known as shifting cultivation.

Generally, the following steps are taken in slash and burn agriculture:

1. Prepare the field by cutting down vegetation; plants that provide food or timber may be left standing.

2. The downed vegetation is allowed to dry until just before the rainiest part of the year to ensure an effective burn.

3. The plot of land is burned to remove vegetation, drive away pests, and provide a burst of nutrients for planting.

4. Planting is done directly in the ashes left after the burn.

Cultivation (the preparation of land for planting crops) on the plot is done for a few years, until the fertility of the formerly burned land is reduced. The plot is left alone for longer than it was cultivated, sometimes up to 10 or more years, to allow wild vegetation to grow on the plot of land. When vegetation has grown again, the slash and burn process may by repeated.

Geography of Slash and Burn Agriculture

Places where open land for farming is not readily available because of dense vegetation are the places where slash and burn agriculture is practiced most often. These regions include central Africa, northern South America, and Southeast Asia, and typically within grasslands and rainforests.

Many critics claim that slash and burn agriculture contributes to a number of reoccurring problems specific to the environment.

Slash and burn is a method of agriculture primarily used by tribal communities for subsistence farming (farming to survive). Humans have practiced this method for about 12,000 years, ever since the transition known as the Neolithic Revolution, the time when humans stopped hunting and gathering and started to stay put and grow crops. Today, between 200 and 500 million people, or up to 7% of the world's population, uses slash and burn agriculture.

When used properly, slash and burn agriculture provides communities with a source of food and income. Slash and burn allows for people to farm in places where it usually is not possible because of dense vegetation, soil infertility, low soil nutrient content, uncontrollable pests, or other reasons.

Negative Aspects of Slash and Burn

Many critics claim that slash and burn agriculture contributes to a number of reoccurring problems specific to the environment. They include:

- Deforestation: When practiced by large populations, or when fields are not given sufficient time for vegetation to grow back, there is a temporary or permanent loss of forest cover.

- Erosion: When fields are slashed, burned, and cultivated next to each other in rapid succession, roots and temporary water storages are lost and unable to prevent nutrients from leaving the area permanently.

- Nutrient Loss: For the same reasons, fields may gradually lose the fertility they once had. The result may be desertification, a situation in which land is infertile and unable to support growth of any kind.

- Biodiversity Loss: When plots of land area cleared, the various plants and animals that lived there are swept away. If a particular area is the only one that holds a particular species, slashing and burning could result in extinction for that species. Because slash and burn agriculture is often practiced in tropical regions where biodiversity is extremely high, endangerment and extinction may be magnified.

The negative aspects above are interconnected, and when one happens, typically another happens also. These issues may come about because of irresponsible practices of slash and burn agriculture by a large amount of people. Knowledge of the ecosystem of the area and agricultural skills could prove very helpful in the safe, sustainable use of slash and burn agriculture.

Genetically Modified Crops Contribute to Biodiversity Loss

Deniza Gertsberg

Deniza Gertsberg is a practicing attorney in the New York City area and the editor and publisher of GMO Journal, a website focused on the health, environmental, and moral impacts of genetically modified foods and ingredients.

It is a statistic that is hard to deny: industrial forms of agriculture, with emphasis on large-scale monoculture crop production, have a negative impact on biodiversity. The Food and Agricultural Organization of the United Nations, referring to the scale of the loss as "extensive," found that some 75 percent of plant genetic diversity has been lost since 1900 as farmers turn to genetically uniform, mass-produced crop varieties.

The term "biodiversity" was derived from "biological" and "diversity," and refers to the total diversity of all life in a given locale—one as small as a backyard (or smaller) or as large as the entire planet Earth.

Since genetically modified crops (a.k.a. GMOs) reinforce genetic homogeneity and promote large scale monocultures, they contribute to the decline in biodiversity and increase vulnerability of crops to climate change, pests and diseases.

The Impact of GMOs on Biodiversity

Genetically modified crops grow in a dynamic environment and interact with other species of the agro-ecosystem and surrounding environment. As "biological novelties to the ecosystems," GM crops may potentially affect the "fitness of other species, population dynamics, ecological roles, and interactions, promoting local extinctions, population explosions, and changes in community structure and function inside and outside agroecosystems."

> *The impact of GMOs on biodiversity is also seen in the development of superweeds and superbugs.*

The recent concerns raised by Dr. Don Huber, who noted a link between GM crops, engineered to withstand continued applications of glyphosate, plant diseases and spontaneous abortions and infertility in pigs, horses, cattle and other livestock, further underscore the troubling fact that GM crops may likely have a larger negative impact on the agroecosystem and the surrounding environment. More importantly, Huber's revelations further point to the inaccurate assumptions made by this nation's regulators. GM crops are not substantially equivalent to their conventional counterparts, they interact in novel ways to impact the plant, the soil and the animals that consume them and government agencies should think twice before deregulating GMOs.

Independent scientists studying the effects of GMOs have also raised other concerns regarding the impact of GMOs on biodiversity. The spread of transgenes to wild or weedy relatives, the impact of GMOs on nontarget organisms (especially weeds or local varieties) through the acquisition of transgenic traits via hybridization, the evolution of resistance to pests (in case of *Bt* crops), accumulation of *Bt* toxins, which remain active in the soil after the crop is plowed under and bind tightly to clays and humic acids and the unanticipated effects of the Bt toxin on nontarget herbivorous insects, are areas of concern as are increasing concerns about the adverse impact of GMOs on insects (such as bees, for example), nematodes, and birds, all of whom either consume GMOs seeds or their by-products or are present in glyphosate saturated soils. "[T]he vast majority of soybeans and cotton, and 70% of our corn, is Roundup Ready, leading to over 230 million lbs of glyphosate being sprayed each year," noted Bill Freese, the Science Policy Analyst at the Center For Food Safety.

Furthermore, the impact of GMOs on biodiversity is also seen in the development of superweeds and superbugs since over-reliance on and the abundant use of single herbicide and pesticide lead to resistance in the pest community. The "unregulated use of glyphosate-resistant crop systems has triggered an epidemic of glyphosate-resistant weeds infesting 10 million acres or more," in this country alone.

GMOs contribute to a decline in biodiversity in one other way. According to Bill Freese, the Science Policy Analyst with the Center For Food Safety, as biotech companies acquire conventional seed companies, conventional and organic seeds are pushed out. Freese states that:

> When Monsanto buys up seed firms, it discontinues the conventional lines, and offers only biotech versions. . . . So from Monsanto's perspective, it makes no sense to sell a high-quality conventional variety when you can charge higher prices and make more money selling that exact same seed, only with a Roundup Ready or other biotech trait(s) stuck into it.

> It's not just Monsanto. Bayer and other biotech firms don't want to sell conventional varieties anymore. [They are] [n]ot as profitable. And since the biotech trait is patented, you get the bonus of patent protection when you insert the trait into a seed. That allows the likes of Monsanto to sue farmers for the "crime" (patent infringement) of saving seed,. . . .

While additional studies are needed to gain a fuller understanding of the impact of GMOs on biodiversity, the currently available information begs the question of whether GMOs bring more harm than good, especially when small-scale farmers, using ecological methods, can address the pressing agricultural concerns.

Commercial Fishing Is a Threat to Marine Biodiversity

Nick Nuttall

Nick Nuttall is a spokesperson for the United Nations Environment Programme (UNEP), an organization that promotes wise use of the environment and sustainable development.

Despite its crucial importance for the survival of humanity, marine biodiversity is in ever-greater danger, with the depletion of fisheries among biggest concerns.

Fishing is central to the livelihood and food security of 200 million people, especially in the developing world, while one of five people on this planet depends on fish as the primary source of protein.

According to UN [United Nations] agencies, aquaculture—the farming and stocking of aquatic organisms including fish, molluscs, crustaceans and aquatic plants—is growing more rapidly than all other animal food producing sectors. But amid facts and figures about aquaculture's soaring worldwide production rates, other, more sobering, statistics reveal that global main marine fish stocks are in jeopardy, increasingly pressured by overfishing and environmental degradation.

"Overfishing cannot continue," warned Nitin Desai, Secretary General of the 2002 World Summit on Sustainable Development, which took place in Johannesburg [South Africa]. "The depletion of fisheries poses a major threat to the food supply of millions of people." The Johannesburg Plan of Implementation calls for the establishment of Marine Protected Areas (MPAs), which many experts believe may hold the key to conserving and boosting fish stocks. Yet, according to the UN Environment Programme's (UNEP) World Conservation Monitoring Centre, in Cambridge, UK [United Kingdom], less than one per cent of the world's oceans and seas are currently in MPAs.

Only a multilateral approach can counterbalance the rate of depletion of the world's fisheries which has increased more than four times in the past 40 years.

A Serious Problem

The magnitude of the problem of overfishing is often overlooked, given the competing claims of deforestation, desertification, energy resource exploitation and other biodiversity depletion dilemmas. The rapid growth in demand for fish and fish products is leading to fish prices increasing faster than prices of meat. As a result, fisheries investments have become more attractive to both entrepreneurs and governments, much to the detriment of small-scale fishing and fishing communities all over the world. In the last decade, in the north Atlantic region, commercial fish populations of cod, hake, haddock and flounder have fallen by as much as 95%, prompting calls for urgent measures. Some are even recommending zero catches to allow for regeneration of stocks, much to the ire of the fishing industry.

According to a Food and Agriculture Organization (FAO) estimate, over 70% of the world's fish species are either fully exploited or depleted. The dramatic increase of destructive fishing techniques worldwide destroys marine mammals and entire ecosystems. FAO reports that illegal, unreported and unregulated fishing worldwide appears to be increasing as fishermen seek to avoid stricter rules in many places in response to shrinking catches and declining fish stocks. Few, if any, developing countries and only a limited number of developed ones are on track to put into effect by this year the International Plan of Action to Prevent, Deter and Eliminate

Unreported and Unregulated Fishing. Despite that fact that each region has its Regional Sea Conventions, and some 108 governments and the European Commission have adopted the UNEP Global Programme of Action for the Protection of the Marine Environment from Land based Activities, oceans are cleared at twice the rate of forests.

The Johannesburg forum stressed the importance of restoring depleted fisheries and acknowledged that sustainable fishing requires partnerships by and between governments, fishermen, communities and industry. It urged countries to ratify the Convention on the Law of the Sea and other instruments that promote maritime safety and protect the environment from marine pollution and environmental damage by ships. Only a multilateral approach can counterbalance the rate of depletion of the world's fisheries which has increased more than four times in the past 40 years.

Genetically Engineered Crops Have Had a Positive Impact on Biodiversity

Janet E. Carpenter

Janet E. Carpenter is an independent consultant based in Massachusetts who has worked with the US Department of Agriculture, the US Agency for International Development, and the National Center for Food and Agricultural Policy.

The potential impact of genetically engineered (GE) crops on biodiversity has been a topic of interest both in general as well as specifically in the context of the Convention on Biological Diversity. In a recent review, I took a biodiversity lens to the substantial body of literature that exists on the potential impacts of GE crops on the environment, considering the impacts at three levels: the crop; farm; and landscape scales. Overall, the review finds that currently commercialized GE crops have reduced the impacts of agriculture on biodiversity, through enhanced adoption of conservation tillage practices, reduction of insecticide use, and use of more environmentally benign herbicides. Increasing yields also alleviate pressure to convert additional land into agricultural use.

Crop Diversity

Crop genetic diversity is considered a source of continuing advances in yield, pest resistance, and quality improvement. It is widely accepted that greater varietal and species diversity would enable agricultural systems to maintain productivity over a wide range of conditions. With the introduction of GE crops, concern has been raised that crop genetic diversity will

Janet E. Carpenter, "Impacts of GE Crops on Biodiversity," *ISB News Report*, June 2011. Reproduced by permission of Information Systems of Biotechnology.

decrease because breeding programs will concentrate on a smaller number of high value cultivars. Three studies have analyzed the impact of the introduction of GE crops on within-crop genetic diversity. Studies of genetic diversity in cotton and soybean in the U.S. both concluded that the introduction of GE varieties was found to have little or no impact on diversity. In contrast, the introduction of Bt [Bacillus thuringiensis, a type of bacteria used as a pesticide] cotton in India initially resulted in a reduction in on-farm varietal diversity due to the introduction of the technology in only a small number of varieties, which has since been offset by more Bt varieties becoming available over time. From a broader perspective, GE crops may actually increase crop diversity by enhancing underutilized alternative crops, making them more suitable for widespread domestication.

The most direct negative impact of agriculture on biodiversity is due to the considerable loss of natural habitats.

Farm-Scale Diversity

Plants have a major influence on soil communities of micro- and other organisms that are fundamental to many functions of soil systems, such as nitrogen cycling, decomposition of wastes, and mobilization of nutrients. The potential impact of Bt crops on soil organisms is well studied. A comprehensive review of the available literature . . . on the effects of Bt crops on soil ecosystems included the results of 70 scientific articles. The review found that, in general, few or no toxic effects of Cry proteins [crystals produced by Bt bacteria] on woodlice, collembolans, mites, earthworms, nematodes, protozoa, and the activity of various enzymes in soil have been reported. Although some effects, ranging from no effect to minor and significant effects, of Bt plants on microbial communities in soil have been reported, they were mostly the result of differences in geography, temperature, plant variety, and soil type and, in general, were transient and not related to the presence of the Cry proteins. Studies published since the . . . review have reached similar conclusions, including novel studies on snails.

Crop production practices also have significant effects on the composition of weed communities. Changes in the kinds of weeds that are important locally are termed weed shifts. Such shifts are particularly relevant for managing weeds in herbicide tolerant crop systems in which tillage practices and herbicide use both play major roles in shaping the weed community. There are reports in the literature of fourteen weed species or groups of closely related species that have increased in abundance in glyphosate resistant (GR) crops. At the same time, in a survey of corn, soybean, and cotton growers in six states, between 36% and 70% of growers indicated that weed pressure had declined after implementing rotations using GR crops.

The use of herbicides can also result in changes to weed communities through the development of herbicide tolerant weed populations. Globally, GR weeds have been confirmed for 21 weeds in 15 countries. Most of these cases have been reported where GR crops are commonly grown. The development of weeds resistant to glyphosate will likely require modification to weed control programs where practices in addition to applying glyphosate are needed to control the resistant populations.

Landscape-Scale Diversity

The most direct negative impact of agriculture on biodiversity is due to the considerable loss of natural habitats, which is caused by the conversion of natural ecosystems into agricultural land. Increases in crop yields allow less land to be dedicated to agriculture than would otherwise be necessary. A large and growing body of literature has shown that the adoption of GE crops has increased yields, particularly in developing countries. A review of the results of global farmer surveys found that the average yield increases for developing countries range from 16% for insect-resistant corn to 30% for insect-resistant cotton, with an 85% yield increase observed in a single study on herbicide-tolerant corn. On average, developed-country farmers report yield increases that range from no change for herbicide-tolerant cotton to a 7% increase for herbicide-tolerant soybean and insect-resistant cotton. Researchers have estimated the benefit of these yield improvements on reducing conversion of land into agricultural use. They estimate that 2.64 million hectares of land would probably be brought into grain and oilseed production if biotech traits were no longer used.

> *The effects of GE crops on above-ground non-target invertebrates have been the subject of a large number of laboratory and field studies.*

The most direct landscape-level effects of growing Bt crops would be expected for target pest species for which the crop is a primary food source and that are mobile across the landscape. Area-wide pest suppression not only reduces losses to adopters of the technology, but may also benefit non-adopters and growers of other crops by reducing crops losses and/or the need to use pest control measures such as insecticides.

Several studies have investigated the impact of the introduction of Bt corn and cotton on regional outbreaks of pest populations, reporting evidence of regional pest suppression in Bt corn and cotton in various areas of the U.S. and in Bt cotton growing regions of China.

The effects of GE crops on above-ground non-target invertebrates have been the subject of a large number of laboratory and field studies. By the end of 2008, over 360 original research papers had been published on non-target effects of

Bt crops. A comprehensive review of the literature . . . included 135 laboratory-based studies on nine Bt crops from 17 countries and 63 field-based studies on five Bt crops from 13 countries, which were analyzed using meta-analysis techniques. In general, laboratory studies identified greater levels of hazard than field studies, at least partially explained by differences in organisms studied, and frequently higher protein exposure in lab studies compared to exposure levels in the field. Field studies demonstrated few harmful non-target effects, with the non-target effects of insecticides being much greater than Bt crops. More recent literature on the non-target impacts of Bt crops are largely consistent with [these] . . . conclusions.

Studies have shown a positive two-way causal relationship between the adoption of conservation tillage and the adoption of GE herbicide tolerant crops.

Studies on the non-target impacts of herbicide tolerant crops, such as the UK [United Kingdom] Farm Scale Evaluations (FSE), have found that the effects on various groups of arthropods followed the effects on the abundance of their resources. Where weed control was more effective, the reduction in weeds and weed seeds led to decreases in insects that live in or on weeds, and vice versa. Other studies on the non-target impacts of herbicide tolerant crops, conducted for HT [herbicide tolerant] soybean and corn in the U.S. and HT canola in Canada, have reached similar conclusions.

The bird survey results of the FSE were in accord with differences in food availability found in the studies. Specifically, a greater abundance of granivores was found on conventional than genetically engineered herbicide tolerant sugar beet, as well as on genetically engineered herbicide tolerant maize after application of herbicides to the GE HT field. No differences were detected in spring oilseed rape. In the subsequent winter season, granivores were more abundant in fields where conventional sugar beet had been grown than on GE HT fields. Several bird species were more abundant on maize stubbles following GE HT treatment.

Indirect Indicators

The introduction of herbicide tolerant crops has been associated with the increased adoption of conservation tillage practices, which decreases run-off, increases water infiltration, and reduces erosion. Trends in the adoption of conservation tillage have been studied in the U.S. and Argentina, the largest growers of herbicide tolerant crops. While conservation tillage was already being adopted by some growers prior to the introduction of GE herbicide tolerant crops in both countries, studies have shown a positive two-way causal relationship between the adoption of conservation tillage and the adoption of GE herbicide tolerant crops. The pest management traits that are embodied in currently commercialized GE crops have led to changes in the use of pesticides that may have impacts on biodiversity. If the planting of GE pest-resistant crop varieties eliminates the need for broad-spectrum insecticidal control of primary pests, naturally occurring control agents are more likely to suppress secondary pest populations, maintaining a diversity and abundance of prey for birds, rodents, and amphibians. In addition to the studies on the non-target impacts of GE crops compared to conventional practices, many studies have quantified changes in pesticide use since the introduction of GE crops. Reductions ranging from 14% to 75% of total active ingredient have been reported for Bt crops compared to conventional crops in Argentina, Australia, China, India, and the U.S.

Fewer surveys have captured changes in herbicide use in GE herbicide tolerant crops, perhaps because the impact of GE herbicide tolerant crops has largely been a substitution between herbicides that are applied at different rates, and therefore, changes in the amount of herbicide used is a poor indicator of environmental impact. Several studies have been done to apply environmental indicators to observed changes in pesticide use related to the adoption of both insect resistant and herbicide tolerant crops, which all show a reduction in the environmental impact of pesticides used on GE crops.

Positive Impacts Overall

Knowledge gained over the past 15 years that GE crops have been grown commercially indicates that the impacts on biodiversity are positive on balance. By increasing yields, decreasing insecticide use, increasing use of more environmentally friendly herbicides, and facilitating adoption of conservation tillage, GE crops have contributed to increasing agricultural sustainability.

Continued yield improvements in crops such as rice and wheat are expected with insect resistant and herbicide tolerant traits.

Previous reviews have also reached the general conclusion that GE crops have had little to no negative impact on the environment. Most recently, the U.S. National Research Council released a comprehensive assessment of the effect of GE crop adoption on farm sustainability in the U.S. that concluded, "[g]enerally, [GE] crops have had fewer adverse effects on the environment than non-[GE] crops produced conventionally".

GE crops can continue to decrease pressure on biodiversity as global agricultural systems expand to feed a world population that is expected to continue to increase for the next 30 to 40 years. Due to higher income elasticities of demand and population growth, these pressures will be greater in developing countries. Both current and pipeline technology hold great potential in this regard. The potential of currently commercialized GE crops to increase yields, decrease pesticide use, and facilitate the adoption of conservation tillage has yet to be realized, as there continue to be countries where there is a good technological fit, but they have not yet approved these technologies for commercialization.

In addition to the potential benefits of expanded adoption of current technology, several pipeline technologies offer additional promise of alleviating the impacts of agriculture on biodiversity. Continued yield improvements in crops such as rice and wheat are expected with insect resistant and herbicide tolerant traits that are already commercialized in other crops.

Technologies such as drought tolerance and salinity tolerance would alleviate the pressure to convert high biodiversity areas into agricultural use by enabling crop production on suboptimal soils. Drought tolerance technology, which allows crops to withstand prolonged periods of low soil moisture, is anticipated to be commercialized within five years. The technology has particular relevance for areas like sub-Saharan Africa, where drought is a common occurrence and access to irrigation is limited. Salt tolerance addresses the increasing problem of saltwater encroachment on freshwater resources.

Nitrogen use efficiency technology is also under development, which can reduce run-off of nitrogen fertilizer into surface waters. The technology promises to decrease the use of fertilizers while maintaining yields, or increase yields achievable with reduced fertilizer rates where access to fertilizer inputs is limited. The technology is slated to be commercialized within the next 10 years.

Agricultural Productivity Does Not Have to Result in Biodiversity Loss

Jonathan Latham and Allison Wilson

Jonathan Latham is executive director of the Bioscience Resource Project, a public interest science organization, and Allison Wilson is the science director and cofounder of the Bioscience Resource Project.

According to conventional wisdom, the Brazilian city of Belo Horizonte (pop. 2.5 million) has achieved something impossible. So, too, has the island of Cuba. They are feeding their hungry populations largely with local, low-input farming methods that enhance the environment rather than degrade it. They have achieved this, moreover, at a time of rising food prices when others have mostly retreated from their own food security goals.

The conventional wisdom contradicted by these examples is that high yielding agricultural systems necessarily reduce biodiversity. Sometimes this assumption is extended to become the 'Borlaug hypothesis' after Norman Borlaug, the architect of the green revolution. The Borlaug hypothesis states that the preservation of rainforests, an example of biodiversity, depends on intensive industrial production of sufficient food to allow for the luxury of unfarmed areas.

So, since Belo Horizonte and Cuba appear to have defied this logic, what is their secret? Are they succeeding in spite of their commitment to sustainability, or because of it? Or is conventional wisdom simply wrong? These pressing questions are explored in a new review, "*Food security and biodiversity:*

Jonathan Latham and Allison Wilson, "How Agriculture Can Provide Food Security Without Destroying Biodiversity," Independent *Science News*, Bioscience Resource Project, May 23, 2011. All rights reserved. Reproduced with permission.

can we have both?" by Michael Jahi Chappell and Liliana La-valle, and published in the journal *Agriculture and Human Values.*

A Pathbreaking New Approach

Whether agricultural productivity and biodiversity are mutually exclusive has only recently emerged as a central question in agriculture. It follows increasing awareness, both that global biodiversity is in rapid decline, and that much of the decline is a result of industrialised agriculture. This is evident from data as diverse as increases in the number and size of ocean dead zones to declines in pollinators.

However, as the number of those who go hungry swells, countries and development advocates see themselves as faced with seemingly impossible choices between food security and environmental degradation. Such pressures, together with the acknowledgment that the productivity of industrialised agriculture can be short-lived, have stimulated academics and others to reexamine their thinking.

> *Biodiversity of every kind is enhanced on farms that avoid industrial methods compared with farms that do not.*

Perhaps the best-known attempt to rigorously evaluate the biodiversity versus food question was the International Assessment of Agricultural Knowledge, Science Technology and Development (IAASTD). This United Nations-sponsored commission was set up to resolve the competing ways forward being offered for agriculture. Reporting in 2007, the IAASTD commission left its mark mainly by pointing out that it is a mistake to think of agriculture as simply about productivity. Agriculture provides employment and livelihoods, it underpins food quality, food safety and nutrition, and it allows food choices and cultural diversity. It is also necessary for water quality, broader ecosystem health, and even carbon sequestration. Agriculture, concluded the IAASTD, should never be reduced merely to a question of production. It must necessarily be integrated with the many needs of humans and ecosystems.

According to John Vandermeer of the University of Michigan, the IAASTD report "did conclude that food security and biodiversity could be reconciled". Amidst discussion of many other issues that conclusion, however, was largely lost. What Chappell and LaValle have contributed, he says, is to focus specifically on the question of whether biodiversity and food security can co-exist in the same place. "They have brought together the data that can resolve the contradictions contained in both sides of the biodiversity versus food argument", he says. Helda Morales, Professor of Agroecology at El Colegio de la Frontera Sur, Mexico, agrees. "This is a careful review of the relevant information available on biodiversity and food security."

Sustainable Agriculture and Productivity

Yields are the first issue Chappell and LaValle considered. Surveying the scientific evidence, they find it supports the idea that a 'hypothetical world alternative agriculture system' could adequately provide for present or even predicted future populations. This is primarily because present and future populations do not need more food than we currently produce. But it is also because agroecological methods involve only a minor yield loss compared with the best that industrial agriculture has to offer. Indeed small farms, which they believe will have to be the basis of any future sustainable agriculture, typically yield more than larger ones. Both conclusions are accepted by Teja Tscharntke, Professor of Agroecology at Georg-August University in Goettingen, Germany. "Hunger in the developing countries can only be reduced by helping smallholders," he says, and even in Germany, "organic farming would easily feed the population if nutritional recommendations were followed".

Sustainable Agriculture and Biodiversity

On the question of whether agroecological methods also enhance biodiversity, the answers appear even more clear cut. While industrialised agriculture is often considered the biggest single global contributor to extinction, biodiversity of every kind is enhanced on farms that avoid industrial methods compared with farms that do not. A recent meta-analysis cited by the review put this figure at "30% more species and 50% more individuals" on agroecological farms. Chappell and La-Valle found that smaller farms using agroecological methods are more biodiverse and less harmful to the environment generally. This finding was consistent over a wide range of localities, crops and production systems. Probably that is because multiple aspects of industrialised agriculture, from large field sizes to the use of nitrogenous fertilisers and pesticides, are each associated with biodiversity losses.

> *The immediate practical obstacle . . . to choosing a food system that supports both food security and the environment is public policy.*

Embedded Agriculture

Agriculture is a system that functions within bigger ecological, political and economic systems. Success, therefore, must ultimately be judged at that level. Chappell and LaValle consider that the two examples they studied—Belo Horizonte and Cuba—offer tentative evidence of success at a regional level. Of these two, Cuba's commitment (and also success) appears to have been the greater. It is claimed, for example that the "capital city of Havana is now almost entirely supplied by alternative agriculture, in or on the periphery of, the city itself". They acknowledge, however, that two examples do not prove anything except a principle. As Teja Scharntke puts it "such examples may be models for some but not all countries."

Future Directions

Nevertheless, say Chappell and LaValle, this all points to the conclusion that "the best solution to both food security and biodiversity problems would be widespread conversion to alternative practices." Instead of supporting a competitive relationship "the evidence emphasizes the interdependence of biodiversity and agriculture." Helda Morales goes even further "I would go beyond this statement and say that we cannot have food security if we do not have biodiversity".

For John Vandermeer, the uniquely holistic approach of Chappell and LaValle is the key to a consensus. "When people dispute these conclusions, it is almost invariably because they are using too narrow a frame of reference." And it is a consensus that appears to be gaining wider attention. In December of 2010 The United Nations special rapporteur on the right to food published a document asserting that agroecology had demonstrated "proven results" and that "the scaling up of these experiences is the main challenge today."

The immediate practical obstacle, however, to choosing a food system that supports both food security and the environment is public policy. Citing Per Pinstrup-Andersen, the former Director General of the International Food Policy Research Institute, Chappell and LaValle state: "It is a myth that the eradication of food insecurity is truly treated as a high priority." The real obstacles to ecological high-yield farming, Vandermeer believes, are research priorities and economics. "Industrial farming only appears to be more viable because it is subsidised." Even though there are at present some uncertainties, "If we applied the same research efforts to agroecological approaches that we currently do to support industrialised farming, even more could be achieved."

Small, Sustainable Farms
Can Help Protect Biodiversity
in Tropical Forests

Sciencedaily

Sciencedaily is a website that offers news and information about science topics.

Conventional wisdom among many ecologists is that industrial-scale agriculture is the best way to produce lots of food while preserving biodiversity in the world's remaining tropical forests. But two University of Michigan [U-M] researchers reject that idea and argue that small, family-owned farms may provide a better way to meet both goals.

The Role of Small Farms in the Tropics

In many tropical zones around the world, small family farms can match or exceed the productivity of industrial-scale operations, according to U-M researchers Ivette Perfecto and John Vandermeer. At the same time, smaller diversified farms are more likely to help preserve biodiversity in tropical regions undergoing massive amounts of deforestation, Perfecto and Vandermeer conclude in a paper to be published online Feb. 22 [2010] in the *Proceedings of the National Academy of Sciences (PNAS)*.

"Most of the tropical forest that's left is fragmented, and what you have are patches of forest surrounded by agriculture," said Perfecto, a professor at the School of Natural Resources and Environment. "If you want to maintain biodiversity in those patches of forest, then the key is to allow organisms to migrate between the patches.

"And small-scale family farms that adopt sustainable agricultural technologies are more likely to favor migration of species than a huge, monocultural plantation of soybeans or sugar cane or some other crop."

An Alternative to Large Farms

Some ecologists have suggested that the history of eastern North American forests provides a preview of what's likely to happen in the tropics. European colonization of eastern North America led to massive deforestation that accompanied the expansion of agriculture. Later, industrialization drew people to cities from the rural areas, and the forests recovered.

Small, family-owned farms that use agroecological techniques come closest to mimicking natural forest habitat, [allowing] plants and animals to migrate between forest fragments.

This scenario is known as the forest transition model. It has been argued that if a similar progression occurs in the tropics, then the decline in rural populations would make more land potentially available for conservation. A corollary of the forest transition model states that if you consolidate agriculture into large, high-tech farms, productivity increases and more land is freed up for conservation. But after reviewing case studies from Costa Rica, El Salvador, Panama, Argentina, Brazil and Mexico, Perfecto and Vandermeer conclude "there is little to suggest that the forest transition model is useful for the tropics" and that it "projects an overly optimistic vision."

Instead, the U-M researchers propose an alternative model, which they call the matrix quality model. They say it provides a solid foundation for conservation planning in tropical regions.

If you think of the fragments of remaining tropical forest as islands in an ocean of agriculture, the ocean is what Perfecto and Vandermeer call the matrix—it's the area between the patches of undisturbed natural habitat. A high-quality matrix is one that enables plants and animals to migrate between the remaining patches of forest, increasing the likelihood that a given species will be able to survive, helping to preserve biodiversity.

Small, family-owned farms that use agroecological techniques come closest to mimicking natural forest habitat, thereby creating corridors that allow plants and animals to migrate between forest fragments. Agroecological techniques can include the use of biological controls instead of pesticides, the use of compost or other organic matter instead of chemical fertilizers, and the use of agroforestry methods, which involve growing crops beneath a canopy of trees or growing crops mixed with fruit trees such as mangoes or avocados.

"If you're really interested in conserving species, you should not just concentrate on preserving the fragments of natural habitat that remain, even though that's where many species are," said Vandermeer, a professor of ecology and evolutionary biology and a professor at the School of Natural Resources and Environment. "You also need to concentrate on the areas between the fragments, because those are the places that species have to migrate through." Vandermeer said he advocates the break-up of large-scale farms in the tropics, as well as incentives to encourage "a large number of small-scale farmers, each managing the land to the best of his or her ability, using agroecological techniques."

Perfecto said these goals are in line with the findings of the 2009 International Assessment of Agricultural Knowledge, Science and Technology for Development synthesis report. The report concluded that small-scale, sustainable farms are the best way to alleviate world hunger while promoting sustainable development. Perfecto was one of the report's authors.

The PNAS article by Perfecto and Vandermeer is part of a special report in the journal about solutions to the world food crisis.

CHAPTER 4

How Can Earth's Biodiversity Be Protected?

Chapter Preface

The main tool in the United States for protecting biodiversity is the Endangered Species Act (ESA)—a federal law enacted by Congress in 1973 to protect threatened and endangered plants and animals and their habitats in the country. The law is enforced by the US Fish and Wildlife Service (FWS) and the US National Oceanic and Atmospheric Administration Fisheries Service (often called the National Marine Fisheries Service). The term *endangered species* refers to species that are likely to become extinct in all or a large part of their range. The term *threatened species* refers to species that are likely to become endangered in the future if no action is taken. The ESA creates lists of protected plant and animal species both nationally and worldwide, and the species contained on these lists are referred to as listed species. As of January 2012, the FWS listed 1,066 plant and animal species as endangered in the United States and 315 species as threatened.

ESA protection is given to species that the FWS and the National Marine Fisheries Service determine to be endangered or threatened. This determination is made after a thorough review of scientific data on the health of the species collected by local, state, and national scientists. Some of the factors considered are whether a large part of the species' habitat has been degraded or destroyed, whether the species is threatened by other human-caused activities, whether the species has been over-exploited by humans, whether the species is suffering from disease or predation, and whether the species is under other legal protections.

If a species is awarded an ESA listing as threatened or endangered, federal law prohibits the plant or animal from being taken—that is, hunted, trapped, captured, collected, harassed, or harmed in any way. Breeding, natural behaviors, and habitats of these species are also protected. The goal is to return the species to a healthy state so that it can be taken off the ESA list. The ESA is considered by most observers to be a highly successful piece of legislation, because it has helped to save, according to some estimates, about 227 species from extinction. Following the passage of the ESA in the United States, the program was replicated by the international community in the Convention on International Trade in Endangered Species of Wild Fauna and Flora (CITES), an international treaty that works to preserve species around the world.

Species that have been saved from extinction thanks to the ESA include such iconic American animals as the bald eagle, gray wolf, and grizzly bear. The bald eagle was almost decimated in the 1960s by pesticides and other chemicals such as DDT that thinned the shells of eagle eggs, killing the young and preventing reproduction. Reduced to only about five hundred, with the help of a DDT ban, breeding programs, and habitat protection, the eagle made a comeback and more than 7,000 breeding pairs are now soaring over the United States. Gray wolves faced a similar fate of near extinction because wolves were poisoned and trapped by ranchers and farmers to protect livestock. Today, thanks to the ESA's work to restore habitat, reintroduce wolves into various regions, and compensate ranchers for livestock losses, wolves have rebounded and now number in the thousands in Minnesota and western states. Excessive hunting and habitat loss also almost eliminated grizzly bears from the United States. Since 1975, however, grizzlies have significantly increased their populations in western national parks, such as Yellowstone and adjacent areas.

The ESA, however, has been very controversial and has been criticized by people who think it protects every threatened species at the expense of economic development. In fact, the original law required that ESA species listings be based solely on scientific considerations about the ability of a species to survive and could not include economic factors such as whether protecting a species will harm construction projects, housing developments, manufacturing, or other economic activities. The ESA was subsequently amended to require that ESA species recovery plans account for economic impact. However, the ESA still gives the federal government significant power to develop recovery plans and designate critical habitat, and very few projects have been completely exempted where they have been shown to harm local listed species.

One famous battle over ESA protections in the 1970s involved the snail darter, a small fish in the Tennessee River that was threatened by a proposal to build a dam in the river. The dam developer sought an exemption from ESA requirements, and the ESA was amended to allow such exemptions, but ultimately the developer was granted the right to build the dam by an act of Congress. In the end, the dam did not cause the snail darter to go extinct, and various efforts have since allowed the fish to be upgraded from endangered to threatened. ESA critics point to this and similar situations as proof that the ESA standards are too high and that they do not adequately consider human needs. Environmentalists typically disagree, arguing that as many species as possible should be saved and that human economic development is already outpacing the ability of the ESA to protect habitat for currently listed endangered and threatened species. In addition, a 2011 study found that the ESA list fails to include hundreds of American species that are considered to be endangered or threatened by the world's leading threatened species list, the IUCN Red List—a list prepared by the International Union for Conservation of Nature (IUCN), a respected international organization. The tension between biodiversity preservation and economic development lies at the heart of the biodiversity debate. The authors of the viewpoints in this chapter suggest other ways that Earth's biodiversity can be protected.

Creating Protected Area Habitats Is a Critical Strategy for Conserving Biodiversity

Convention on Biological Diversity

The Convention on Biological Diversity is an international agreement signed by one hundred and sixty-eight countries, dedicated to promoting sustainable development and preserving biodiversity.

Protected areas are the cornerstone of biodiversity conservation; they maintain key habitats, provide refugia, allow for species migration and movement, and ensure the maintenance of natural processes across the landscape. Not only do protected areas secure biodiversity conservation, they also secure the well-being of humanity itself. Protected areas provide livelihoods for nearly 1.1 billion people, are the primary source of drinking water for over a third of the world's largest cities and are a major factor in ensuring global food security. Well managed protected areas harbouring participatory and equitable governance mechanisms yield significant benefits far beyond their boundaries, which can be translated into cumulative advantages across a national economy and contribute to poverty reduction and sustainable development including achievement of the Millennium Development Goals [international development goals set for the year 2015]. As the detrimental impact of climate change threatens the planet, protected areas provide a convenient solution to an inconvenient truth. Better managed, better connected, better governed and better financed protected areas are recognized as the key to both mitigation and adaptation responses to climate change.

The CBD Programme of Work on Protected Areas and Progress in Its Implementation

In February 2004, the CBD [Convention on Biological Diversity, an international agreement on biodiversity] parties made the most comprehensive and specific protected area commitments ever made by the international community by adopting the Programme of Work on Protected Areas (PoWPA). The PoWPA enshrines development of participatory, ecologically representative and effectively managed national and regional systems of protected areas, where necessary stretching across national boundaries. From designation to management, the PoWPA can be considered as a defining framework or "blueprint" for protected areas for the coming decades. It is a framework for cooperation between Governments, donors, NGOs [nongovernmental organizations] and local communities, for without such collaboration, programmes cannot be successful and sustainable over the long-term.

> *Governments are increasingly likely to consider protected areas as a strategic investment in their national economies.*

To date, there are many signs of progress and there is much to celebrate. Political will and commitments are clearly being catalyzed. A recent summary of global implementation of the Programme of Work found that since 2004, nearly 6,000 new protected areas have been established, covering more than 60 million hectares. There are now about 130,000 protected areas, covering nearly 13% of the world's terrestrial surface, and over 6% of territorial marine areas. Many of these are embedded in comprehensive national and regional networks of connected protected areas and corridors.

While these are commendable achievements, there are still some areas that are lagging behind. The social costs and benefits, the effective participation of indigenous and local communities and the diversification of various governance types need more commitment and resolute actions. The evaluation and improvement of management effectiveness, and the development and implementation of sustainable finance plans with diversified portfolios of traditional and innovative financial mechanisms need enhanced measures. Climate change considerations for both mitigation and adaptation responses need to be incorporated. Strengthening implementation of PoWPA will require concerted efforts and the combined strength of all sectors of society, as well as alliances at national, regional and international levels between policy makers, civil society, indigenous and local communities and business and the private sector.

Looking Ahead

Governments are increasingly likely to consider protected areas as a strategic investment in their national economies—a recent report estimates that investments in creating and managing protected areas will yield returns in societal benefits on the order of 25:1 to 100:1. Governments are also likely to view protected areas as a fundamental strategy to not only conserve biodiversity, but also to achieve the Millennium Development Goals, secure vital ecosystem services, support local livelihoods, and enable humans and nature alike to adapt to the impacts of climate change.

Setting Aside Protected Habitats Will Not Stop Biodiversity Loss

Tom Zeller

Tom Zeller is a senior writer for The Huffington Post, *an online news magazine and website.*

Despite rapid and substantial growth in the amount of land and sea designated as protected habitat over the last four decades, the diversity of species the world over is plummeting, a new study has found.

Over 100,000 so-called "protected areas" representing some 7 million square miles of land and nearly 1 million square miles of ocean have been established since the 1960's, noted the analysis, published Thursday [July 28, 2011] in the journal *Marine Ecology Progress Series*.

And yet, according to a widely cited index used to track planetary biodiversity, the wealth of terrestrial and marine species has seen steady decline over roughly the same period, suggesting that simply protecting swaths of land and sea—a common conservation strategy worldwide—is inadequate for preventing the steady disappearance of earth's creatures.

"The problem is bigger than one we can realistically solve with protected areas—even if they work under the best conditions," said Camilo Mora, an assistant professor in the Department of Geography at the University of Hawaii at Manoa and lead author of the study. "The protected area approach is expensive and requires a lot of political and human capital," Dr. Mora continued in an email message to *The Huffington Post*.

"Our suggestion is that we should redirect some of those resources to deal with ultimate solutions." . . .

Too Many Stressors on Biodiversity

The steady loss of biodiversity—defined roughly as the rich variety of living things—can, in turn, have profound implications for human civilization, which relies on healthy, variegated ecosystems to provide a host of ecological services from water filtration and oxygen generation to food, medicine, clothing and fuel.

The precise value of such services is difficult to quantify, but one economic analysis estimated they were worth as much as $33 trillion globally.

Researchers . . . suggest that the implementation of habitat protection is unable to keep pace with other stressors contributing to species loss overall.

While the study concedes that individual protected areas that are well-designed and well-managed can be successful in preventing the imminent extinction of species and ecosystems, a variety of other forces conspire to further reduce biodiversity overall.

"Protected areas, as usually implemented, can only protect from over-exploitation, and from habitat destruction due to exploitation and other direct human actions within their borders. They are a tool for regulating human access and extraction," said Peter F. Sale, assistant director of the United Nations University Institute for Water, Environment and Health, and the study's co-author. "Biodiversity loss is also caused by pollution, by arrival of invasive species, by decisions to convert habitat to other uses—farms, villages, cities—and by various components of climate change," he told *HuffPost*. "None of these are mitigated by the creation of protected areas except, possibly, the removal of habitat to other uses."

In other words, the researchers, who based their analysis on a broad range of global data and a review of existing literature, suggest that the implementation of habitat protection is unable to keep pace with other stressors contributing to species loss overall.

This is partly due to lack of enforcement. Only about 5.8 percent of terrestrial protected areas and 0.08 percent of marine sanctuaries see reliable and consistent enforcement.

Too Slow a Pace

Further, the authors note most research suggests that between 10 percent and 30 percent of the world's ecosystems need to be protected to preserve optimal biodiversity. But despite what appears to be a rapid increase in protected lands, the pace is too slow to achieve those targets anytime soon. On land, the 10 percent target, under the best of circumstances, would not be reached until 2043, the study estimated. The 30 percent target would not be achieved until 2197. The same target percentages for marine sanctuaries would be reached by 2067 and 2092, respectively.

And these projections are almost certainly too optimistic, the authors note, because the rate of establishment of new protected areas would be expected to slow considerably as conservation efforts run up against the needs of a rapidly expanding human population.

Reversing biodiversity losses will require a vast rethinking of conservation strategy.

From the study:

[D]emand on marine fisheries is projected to increase by 43 percent by 2030 to supply ongoing food demands, while projected CO_2 emissions by 2050 are expected to severely impact [more than] 80 percent of the world's coral reefs and affect marine fish communities globally, causing local extinctions and facilitating invasions resulting in changes in species composition of up to 60 percent. On land, the growing human population and demand for housing, food and energy are expected to substantially increase the intensity of stressors associated with the conversion of land cover to agriculture and urbanization, e.g. the release of nutrients and other pollutants, climate warming and altered precipitation. In short, the extent of coverage by [protected areas] is still limited and is growing at a slower rate than that at which biodiversity threats are developing.

Global population is expected to pass 7 billion in October [2011], according to new estimates from the population division of the Department of Economic and Social Affairs at the United Nations. That's an increase of 1 billion people in about a dozen years.

Other Challenges

Other challenges include the size of protected areas—which are often too small for larger species to survive—and the lack of connectivity between protected areas, which is needed for healthy genetic dispersal.

The authors of Thursday's analysis suggest that reversing biodiversity losses will require a vast rethinking of conservation strategy—one that redirects limited resources toward more holistic solutions. This would include efforts to reduce human population growth—and its attending consumption patterns—as well as the deployment of technologies that would increase the productivity of agriculture and aquaculture to meet human needs.

Also needed, the authors wrote: a continued "restructuring of world views to bring them in line with a world of finite resources."

Dr. Sale said, "In the final analysis, we have to recognize that we are pushing up against limits set by the way the biosphere functions. Biodiversity loss is one sign of this."

Sustainable Agriculture Is the Key to Preserving Biodiversity

Annik Dollacker and Juan Gonzalez-Valero

Annik Dollacker is head of International Affairs and Sustainability at Bayer CropScience, one of the world's largest crop science companies; Juan Gonzalez-Valero is responsible for public policy and partnerships at Syngenta International AG, a large global Swiss agribusiness company. Dollacker and Gonzalez-Valero represent their companies at the Ecosystems Focus Area at the World Business Council for Sustainable Development (WBCSD), an organization of companies promoting a sustainable future for business, society, and the environment.

Agriculture is one of the key motors of the global economy. It is a source of foods, fibers and, increasingly, fuel. It provides livelihoods and subsistence for the largest number of people worldwide. It is vital to rural development and therefore critical to poverty alleviation. Cultivated land, including arable lands and shifting cultivation, covers approximately 24% of the world's land area. Partly or fully irrigated agriculture claims 70% of the world's developed fresh water supplies. Today, agriculture accounts for over 38% of global employment.

Biodiversity and the ecosystem services it supports are crucial for successful agriculture. Agriculture relies on biodiversity for pollination, the creation of genetically diverse plant and crop varieties, development of robust, insect or disease-resistant strains, crop protection and watershed control. In short, agriculture has a high level of dependence on the whole range of ecosystem services.

Competition Between Agriculture and Biodiversity

It is estimated that a significant amount of the world's wild biodiversity is found in or around agricultural landscapes. Historically, agriculture served to attract and create new strains of biodiversity. It led to the creation of new plant and seed strains, attracted new animal species and fashioned fresh habitats for biodiversity. Together agriculture, biodiversity and ecosystems constitute a finely interwoven mesh of cross-cutting impacts and challenges. Today, they face a plethora of common threats. Climate change is driving species loss and leading to desertification. Likewise, a growth in the number of alien invasive species is threatening biodiversity and compromising agricultural produce. At the same time, demands on agriculture and pressure on biodiversity are forcing the two into competition.

> *Biodiversity is fundamental to agriculture, food production and sustainable development.*

The last 150 years have witnessed large-scale conversion of land to make way for agricultural and other activities to address demand from the growing world population. Land-use change has both positive and negative impacts. Biodiversity can benefit from agriculture. Making land productive often helps to attract greater biodiversity, while conversion of land for agro-forestry also encourages greater levels of biodiversity. By that same token, negatives can become positives, land that was once considered unproductive because it lacked the necessary nutrients for crop production, often supports a high number of species; this is now widely acknowledged as very important. But deforestation, for example, to make way for agricultural activities has been a significant driver of biodiversity and ecosystem loss.

Global agriculture is under tremendous pressure. Population growth alone is not solely responsible for driving demand for food and non-food crops. As populations are becoming wealthier, consumption patterns are changing and demand for protein such as meat and milk products is going up. The production of 1 kg of chicken meat requires 2 kg of grain, for example, which further amplifies the demand on grain, not to mention increased demand for virtual water. It is estimated that world cereal stocks are currently at their lowest peacetime levels for more than two decades. Similarly, rural-urban migration is reducing the availability of agricultural labor. The UN (United Nations) Population Division estimates that, for the first time, the global urban population has outstripped the rural one, putting greater pressure on farmers to increase production to feed urban populations. In addition, the quest for carbon-neutral energy sources, as well as water scarcity, global food sourcing, fluctuating commodity prices and disproportionate government support to agricultural investment all collude to put further pressure on ecosystems and biodiversity.

Biodiversity is fundamental to agriculture, food production and sustainable development. For innovation in seeds, biodiversity is the crucial 'raw material'. Therefore, biodiversity loss represents a significant business risk. The agricultural sector and the down-stream value chain—food, biochemistry, pharmaceutical, and textile industries—are particularly vulnerable. They face operational risks, including diminishing supplies or rising costs of key resources and inputs, such as raw materials and water, for example. Other potential challenges include governmental restrictions on access to biodiversity; damaged reputations and licenses to operate if public expectations are not met; and potentially restricted access to capital as the financial community adopts more rigorous lending and investment policies.

As the world's population continues to grow, with the knock-on effects this will have on requirements for land (for building and other uses), and demand for renewable resources to counter climate change continues to rise, it would be unrealistic to set past species diversity on cultivated land as a desired target. This level of ambition ignores not only the source and origin of this 'diversity', but also generally the fundamental requirements of sustainable development, biodiversity and ecosystems.

The agricultural sector possesses a wealth of biodiversity-relevant knowledge and therefore has tremendous scope for the effective management of ecosystems and biodiversity resources.

As overall land is limited and further encroachment into pristine habitats not sustainable either, agriculture has to be made more effective and sustainable on the land already cropped. This realization is not altogether recent. In the past 50 years, without the use of ever-improving agricultural technologies (seeds, crop protection products, fertilizers, mechanization, irrigation, *etc.*) a landmass of the size of North America would have had to be turned into farmland. Post war needs shaped agricultural policy which tended towards increased productivity at the expense of wildlife and agro-ecosystem sustainability. Integrated technology knowledge only really came into its own in the 1980s and 1990s.

Sustainable Agriculture

The major challenge today therefore is to secure and increase agricultural yield while at the same time conserving biodiversity, ecosystems, and resources as well as maintaining a healthy base for those who rely on agriculture for their livelihoods. In other words, balancing agricultural productivity with the needs of ecosystems and biodiversity to ensure they are all able to deliver their services in a sustainable manner.

The key to achieving this lies in the implementation of sustainable agriculture. This more holistic and systemic approach integrates the three pillars of sustainability: profitability, environmental protection and social equity. It includes the premise that agriculture needs to be managed while supporting biodiversity and ecosystem health. Integrated Crop Management (ICM) strategies that are being implemented include, among others, setting biodiversity conservation goals for farmland, such as maintaining or enhancing wildlife habitats. Similarly, low-till, and conservation agriculture are also widely promoted approaches. Low-tillage avoids plowing the soil. Not only does this circumvent the use of carbon-emitting fossil fuels that accompanies tractor plowing, this approach—often facilitated by herbicides—also helps avoid soil erosion and improves water retention, by maintaining more organic material in the soil.

The agricultural sector possesses a wealth of biodiversity-relevant knowledge and therefore has tremendous scope for the effective management of ecosystems and biodiversity resources. Farmers are the stewards of the agricultural landscape, its supporting ecosystems and biodiversity.

Crucially, business has a vital role to play in achieving agricultural sustainability. Particularly, those companies in the bio-crop and agricultural sectors can deliver solutions that make agriculture more effective. Some WBCSD [World Business Council for Sustainable Development] member companies are continuously working to develop crop technologies that make agricultural production more effective while respecting biodiversity. Available solutions include energy and water-efficient irrigation techniques, energy-efficient harvesting mechanisms, *etc.* Similarly, green biotechnology solutions for new traits of seeds (higher yields and quality) and crop protection technologies will also help to achieve biodiversity and ecosystem-related objectives.

Market Mechanisms

Market mechanisms too may help achieve sustainable agricultural production and exploitation; particularly for companies further down the value chain that rely indirectly on agriculture and agricultural products. Examples include paying farmers for the supply of ecosystem services such as field margin management, watershed protection or planting cover crops to prevent soil erosion. Trading environmental liabilities such as carbon emissions, wetland mitigation credits, or even biodiversity restoration credits may provide incentives for sustainable consumption. Finally, the use of certification schemes for sustainable production practices could also result in biodiversity and ecosystem gains as well as offer profitable business opportunities for farmers. These may prove essential if integration of biodiversity enhancements into agro-ecosystems is to yield positive results.

To advance the goal of encouraging agriculture which protects or enhances biodiversity, there is a compelling need to devise workable market mechanisms to quantify and monetize the economic value of agriculture's ecosystem services for the beneficiaries of those services.

Many companies, both in the agricultural sector and further down the value chain, are willing to make the investments and develop the technologies and approaches to contribute towards sustainable agriculture as witnessed by the number of business-led initiatives established to standardize certification procedures and environmental standards. However, to do so they need to gain an economic return on investment and therefore rely on supportive science-based policy frameworks and Intellectual Property Rights (IPRs).

Governments need to set targets and provide the necessary policy and market frameworks. However, such targets will remain moot if adequate enforcement mechanisms are not in place. Similarly, any policy framework needs to be properly integrated across a wide variety of sectors and technologies, as well as regions, to ensure that it does not create perverse or counter-incentives. Business and many leading non-governmental organizations are ready to work with governments to achieve these objectives.

The World Must Move Faster to Conserve Tropical Rainforests

The Economist

The Economist is a weekly newspaper focusing on international politics and business news and opinion, based in the United Kingdom.

The summer dry-season, now drawing to an end, is when the Amazon rainforest gets cut and burned. The smoke this causes can often be seen from space. But not this year. Brazil's deforestation rate has dropped astoundingly fast. In 2004 some 2.8m hectares (10,700 square miles) of the Amazon were razed; last year [2009] only around 750,000 hectares were.

This progress is not isolated. Many of the world's biggest clearers of trees have started to hug them. Over the past decade, the UN [United Nations] records, nearly 8m hectares of forest a year were allowed to re-grow or were planted anew. This was mostly in richer places, such as North America and in Europe, where dwindling rural populations have taken the pressure off forestland. But a couple of big poorer countries, notably China, have launched huge tree-planting schemes in a bid to prevent deforestation-related environmental disasters. Even in tropical countries, where most deforestation takes place, Brazil is not alone in becoming more reluctant to chop down trees.

The progress made in recent years shows that mankind is not doomed to strip the planet of its forest cover. But the transition from tree-chopper to tree-hugger is not happening fast enough. Over the past decade, according to UN figures, around 13m hectares of forestland—an area the size of England—was converted each year to other uses, mostly agriculture. If the world is to keep the protective covering that helps it breathe, waters its crops, keeps it cool and nurtures its biodiversity, it is going to have to move fast.

Clearing forests may enrich those who are doing it, but over the long run it impoverishes the planet as a whole.

A Bad Old Habit

For at least 10,000 years, since the ice last retreated and forests took back the earth, people have destroyed them. In medieval Europe an exploding population and hard-working monks put paid to [that is, destroyed] perhaps half its temperate oak and beech woods—mostly, as is usually the case, to clear space for crops. Some 100m hectares of America's forests went in the 19th century, in an arboreal slaughter similarly reinforced by a belief in the godliness of thus "improving" the land. That spirit survives. It is no coincidence that George Bush junior, one of America's more god-fearing presidents, relaxed by clearing brush.

In most rich countries the pressure on forests has eased; but in many tropical ones—home to around half the remaining forest, including the planet's green rainforest girdle—the demand for land is increasing as populations rise. In Congo, which has more rainforest than any country except Brazil, the clearance is mostly driven by smallholders, whose number is about to double. Rising global demand for food and biofuels adds even more to the heat. So will climate change. That may already be happening in Canada, where recent warm winters have unleashed a plague of bark beetles, and in Australia, whose forests have been devastated by drought and forest fires.

Clearing forests may enrich those who are doing it, but over the long run it impoverishes the planet as a whole. Rainforests are an important prop to continental water-cycles. Losing the Amazon rainforest could reduce rainfall across the Americas, with potentially dire consequences for farmers as far away as Texas. By regulating run-off, trees help guarantee water-supplies and prevent natural disasters, like landslides and floods. Losing the rainforest would mean losing millions of species; forests contain 80% of terrestrial biodiversity. And for those concerned about the probable effects of climate change, forests contain twice as much carbon as the atmosphere, in plant-matter and the soils they cover, and when they are razed and their soils disturbed most is emitted. If the Amazon went up in smoke—a scenario which a bit more clearance and a bit more warming makes conceivable—it would spew out more than a decade's worth of fossil-fuel emissions.

Reddy, Steady, Grow

Economic development both causes deforestation and slows it. In the early stages of development people destroy forests for a meagre living. Globalisation is speeding up the process by boosting the demand for agricultural goods produced in tropical countries. At the same time, as people in emerging countries become more prosperous, they start thinking about issues beyond their family's welfare; their governments begin to pass and slowly enforce laws to conserve the environment. Trade can also allow the greener concerns of rich-world consumers to influence developing-world producers.

The transition from clearing to protecting, however, is occurring too slowly. The main international effort to speed it up is an idea known as REDD (Reducing Emissions from Deforestation and Forest Degradation), which pays people in developing countries to leave trees standing. This is not an outlandish concept. It is increasingly common for governments and companies to pay for forest and other ecosystem services. To protect its watershed, New York pays farmers in the Catskills not to develop their land. REDD schemes aspire to do this on a much larger scale. The only notable success of the Copenhagen climate-change conference last year was a commitment to pursue them. Half a dozen rich countries, including Norway, America and Britain, have promised $4.5 billion for starters.

The difficulties are immense. REDD projects will be effective only in places where the government sort-of works, and the tropical countries with the most important forests include some of the world's worst-run places. Even in countries with functioning states, some of the money is bound to be stolen. Yet with sufficient attention to monitoring, verification and, crucially, making sure the cash goes to the people who can actually protect the forest, REDD could work. That will cost much more than has so far been pledged. The most obvious source of extra cash is the carbon market, or preferably a carbon tax. Since saving forests is often the cheapest way to tackle carbon emissions, funding it this way makes sense.

With global climate-change negotiations foundering, the prospects of raising cash for REDD that way look poor. But the money must be found from somewhere. Without a serious effort to solve this problem, the risk from climate change will be vastly increased and the planet will lose one of its most valuable, and most beautiful, assets. That would be a tragedy.

Strong Measures Must Be Taken Soon to Prevent Overfishing in Our Oceans

Save Our Seas Foundation

Save Our Seas Foundation is a nonprofit organization dedicated to protecting our oceans by funding research, education, awareness, and conservation projects focusing on the major threats to the marine environment.

Overfishing occurs when fish and other marine species are caught faster than they can reproduce. It is the result of growing demand for seafood around the world, combined with poor management of fisheries and the development of new, more effective fishing techniques. If left unchecked, it will destroy the marine ecosystem and jeopardise the food security of more than a billion people for whom fish are a primary source of protein.

Sustainable Fishing

The statistics are grim: 3/4 of the world's fish stocks are being harvested faster than they can reproduce. Eighty percent are already fully exploited or in decline. Ninety percent of all large predatory fish—including tuna, sharks, swordfish, cod and halibut—are gone. Scientists predict that if current trends continue, world food fisheries could collapse entirely by 2050.

The most prized species are already disappearing. The 1990s saw the widely-publicised collapse of several major cod fisheries, which have failed to recover even after fishing was stopped. WWF predicts that the breeding population of Atlantic bluefin tuna—one of the ocean's largest and fastest predators, and sought-after as a delicacy used for sushi—will disappear within three years unless catches are drastically reduced.

Modern fishing vessels catch staggering amounts of unwanted fish and other marine life.

As fish populations closer to shore dwindle, commercial fishing operations have shifted their focus to largely unregulated deep-sea fisheries—as much as 40 percent of the world's trawling grounds are now in waters deeper than 200 meters. In doing so, they target species which are particularly vulnerable to overexploitation, like the orange roughy. Like many other deep-sea fish, this species matures late and lives very long—over 150 years. Its low fecundity means populations become depleted more quickly than inshore species when they are overfished, and take much longer to recover. Indeed, many orange roughy stocks have already collapsed, and recently discovered substitute stocks are also rapidly dwindling.

The good news is that areas with competent fisheries management and coast guard policing, mainly in the developed world, have experienced some dramatic recoveries of fish populations. The bad news is that most overfishing takes place in the waters of poor countries where there is no adequate regulation or policing; areas where rogue fleets—some of which hail from developed countries—equipped with high-tech ships can poach without consequences. Using methods like bottom trawling and long-lining, these fleets are capable of wiping out entire fisheries in a single season. And they don't just catch the fish they target.

Bycatch

Modern fishing vessels catch staggering amounts of unwanted fish and other marine life. It's estimated that anywhere from 8 to 25 percent of the total global catch is discarded, cast overboard either dead or dying. That's up to 27 million tonnes of fish thrown out each year—the equivalent of 600 fully-laden Titanics. And the victims aren't just fish. Every year, an estimated 300,000 whales, dolphins and porpoises die entangled in fishing nets, along with thousands of critically-endangered sea turtles. Long-line fisheries also kill huge numbers of seabirds. Over 100,000 Albatrosses die this way every year, and many species are endangered as a result of bycatch.

All modern forms of commercial fishing produce bycatch, but shrimp trawling is by far the most destructive: it is responsible for a third of the world's bycatch, while producing only 2% of all seafood.

Shrimp (and many deep-sea fish) are caught using a fishing method called bottom trawling, which usually involves dragging a net between two trawl doors weighing several tons each across the ocean bed. This has a destructive impact on seabed communities, particularly on fragile deep water coral—a vital part of the marine ecosystem that scientists are just beginning to understand. The effect of bottom trawling on the seafloor has been compared to forest clear-cutting, and the damage it causes can be seen from space. The UN [United Nations] Secretary General reported in 2006 that 95 percent of damage to seamount ecosystems worldwide is caused by deep sea bottom trawling.

Remedies

What can be done? The next few years will be pivotal for the oceans. If strong measures are implemented now, much of the damage can still be reversed. In terms of what needs to happen, preventing overfishing is fairly straightforward: first and foremost, scientifically-determined limits on the number of fish caught must be established for individual fisheries, and these limits must be enforced. Second, fishing methods responsible for most bycatch must either be modified to make them less harmful, or made illegal. And third, key parts of the ecosystem, such as vulnerable spawning grounds and coral reefs, must be fully protected.

In practical terms, this means:

- Putting pressure on governments to limit fishing subsidies, estimated at tens of billions of dollars per year. Eliminating subsidies of this scale lowers the financial incentives to continuously expand fishing fleets far beyond sustainability.

- Establishing and expanding Marine Protected Areas (MPAs), areas of the ocean where natural resources are protected and fishing is either restricted or banned altogether (no-take areas). Presently, 1% of the oceans are MPAs. This number needs to be bigger if they are to help reverse the damage done by overfishing. The Save Our Seas Foundation has been actively involved in supporting MPAs through our projects in the Cocos (Keeling) Island and the Maldives.

- Better monitoring and policing of the fish trade. Pirate fishing continues to grow in scope, and though illegal, fish caught in such operations often end up on our plates.

- Consumers choosing to buy sustainably-sourced seafood and avoiding threatened species. Overfishing is driven by global demand—lowering the demand will lower the damage.

Addressing Biodiversity Loss Will Require More Political Will and Resources

Elizabeth Pennisi

Elizabeth Pennisi is a staff writer and editor for Science *magazine, where she focuses primarily on such issues as genomics, evolution, microbiology, and organismal biology.*

In 2002, 191 nations pledged to significantly reduce the rate of biodiversity loss around the world by 2010. Despite the promises, enshrined in the Convention on Biological Diversity, the plight of threatened species has gotten worse, not better, researchers report online today in *Science*. "All the evidence indicates that governments have failed to deliver on their commitments, and we have failed to meet the 2010 target," says Matthew Walpole, a co-author of the report from the United Nations Environment Programme's World Conservation Monitoring Centre in Cambridge, United Kingdom.

This somber but not unexpected news comes on the eve of a May [2010] meeting of scientists charged with coming up with the convention's goals for the next decade. Those goals will be submitted for approval at a summit of nations in Japan in October. Some experts hope the bad marks will prompt greater commitment to the protection of biodiversity in the next decade. "We have not made a lot of progress, and we need to get our act together," says Thomas Lovejoy, a biodiversity specialist at the Heinz Center, an environmental think tank in Washington, D.C.

Measuring Biodiversity Loss

The new report is a product of the 2010 Biodiversity Indicators Partnership, a consortium of 40 organizations that contributed data and analyses for 31 indicators of biodiversity. The list includes a variety of measures of biodiversity; of the pressures leading to the loss of species, genetic diversity, populations, and ecosystems; of the responses by governments and other organizations; and of the benefits or services provided by biodiversity.

One indicator, the Living Planet Index, for example, compiles thousands of annual population surveys of vertebrates from around the world. It showed a decline of 30% in vertebrate populations since 1970. Other surveys show that the extent of mangroves and sea grasses has shrunk by 20%. Living coral cover is 40% of what it once was. The Red List Index, which keeps tabs on threatened organisms, showed that these species face an increased risk of extinction. Meanwhile, threats, such as deforestation, invasive species, and pollution have increased.

There has been some progress. In the 1970s, Brazil's Amazon had just one national park and one national forest; now, 57% of the land is under some protection, says Lovejoy. The Alliance for Zero Extinction, a consortium of more than 60 organizations that identified 560 places where species are at risk of imminent extinction, found that 40% of the sites are now being preserved to some degree. "This shows that conservation action can and does work," particularly at the local level, says Thomas Brooks of NatureServe, a consortium based in Arlington, Virginia, that collects biodiversity data. "We just need much more of it, and over much longer periods."

The Need for More Political Will and Resources

The study has highlighted the need for better goal-setting. "Slowing the rate of biodiversity loss wasn't a good target," says Benjamin Skolnik, a conservation biologist at the American Bird Conservancy in Washington, D.C. "It wasn't rigorous enough." Delegates to the May meeting are coming up with 20 targets for 2020 and are trying to make them much more concrete and measurable. Some tentative goals include eliminating overfishing, preventing extinctions, and setting aside 15% of the land and sea as protected areas.

Despite the bad news, Walpole's colleague and lead author Stuart Butchart of Birdlife International in Cambridge is optimistic. "We can look after nature if we apply real political will and adequate resources," he says. "2010 must be the year that governments start to take the issue seriously."

Individuals Can Also Take Steps to Protect Biodiversity

Renee Cho

Renee Cho is a freelance environmental writer who has written for various environmental publications. She also is a staff blogger for the Earth Institute, a research institute at Columbia University focused on sustainable development and poverty issues.

Biodiversity—the variety of all living organisms including ecosystems, plants, animals, their habitats and genes—is fundamental to life on Earth. We need biodiversity for its invaluable ecosystem services, providing oxygen, food, clean water, fertile soil, medicines, shelter, protection from storms and floods, a stable climate and recreation. Tragically, today biodiversity is disappearing at 1,000 times the normal rate due to human civilization. Individual species are being obliterated by habitat loss and degradation, invasive species, the spread of pollution and disease, climate change and the over exploitation of resources. And because the human population, which has doubled since 1970, is expected to reach 9 billion by 2050, the biodiversity crisis will only get worse as more people consume more resources.

What can we as individuals do to help slow the loss of biodiversity? Since consumption of resources is a root cause of biodiversity loss, we can consume less and be more mindful about what we consume. We need to leverage our purchasing power to help protect biodiversity by consuming products that do not harm the environment. Ecolabels enable consumers to determine which products are green, safe, and environmentally sustainable. But because so many ecolabels have

Renee Cho, "What You Can Do to Protect Biodiversity," Earth Institute, April 30, 2011. Renee Cho for the Earth Institute. This article was originally published on the State of the Planet—blogs.ei.columbia.edu.

sprung up—in 2010, there were 400 different sustainability certifications available around the world—they can be confusing. Here are some of the most reliable and respected ecolabels to look for.

Green Seal boasts one of the first environmental certification programs.

USDA Organic—The USDA [US Department of Agriculture] Organic seal, given out by the U.S. Department of Agriculture, certifies that raw, fresh and processed products are either 100 percent organic or "organic" (containing 95 percent organically produced ingredients). Organic crops must be raised without conventional pesticides, petroleum-based fertilizers, or sewage sludge-based fertilizers. Animals must be fed organic feed, have access to the outdoors, and cannot be given antibiotics or growth hormones. Genetic engineering is prohibited. Generally, all natural (non-synthetic) substances are allowed in organic production and all synthetic substances are prohibited. Personal care and cosmetic products can also be labeled organic if they meet USDA/National Organic Program criteria.

Fair Trade Certified—This label guarantees that farmers and workers that produce products in the developing world are getting a fair deal. It also ensures protection of local ecosystems and promotes sustainable and organic agriculture. Fair Trade certified products include beans and grains, cocoa, coffee, flowers and plants, fruits and vegetables, honey, herbs and spices, nuts and oil seeds, sugar, tea and wine. Apparel, sports balls, and beauty products can also be certified.

Marine Stewardship Council—The MSC is a global organization that develops standards for sustainable fishing and certifies seafood (from wild capture fisheries only) that comes from sustainable fisheries. At sustainable fisheries, current catches must be maintained at levels that ensure fish populations and their ecosystems remain healthy and productive today and in the future. MSC provides a list of certified sustainable fish for responsible eating.

Green Seal—Established in 1989, Green Seal boasts one of the first environmental certification programs. It uses lifecycle based sustainability standards to certify products, services, and companies that protect the environment and human health. All significant environmental and social impacts are considered, from raw materials extraction through manufacturing to use and disposal. Certified products include cleansers, construction materials, paints, paper, paper towels and tissue, food packaging, and hand soaps. Cleaning services, restaurants and hotels are also certified.

Energy Star—Originally created by the U.S. Department of Environmental Protection and the Department of Energy, Energy Star is now an international standard for energy efficient products. Certified products must perform to consumers' expectations while providing increased energy efficiency, and if an Energy Star product costs more than a traditional equivalent, consumers must be able to recoup their investment in a reasonable amount of time through energy savings. Energy Star products include appliances (refrigerators, washers, dryers, etc.), computers and electronics, lighting and fans, plumbing, heating and cooling equipment, and building products (windows, doors, roofing, insulation, etc.).

Forest Stewardship Council [FSC]—The FSC promotes the sustainable management of the world's forests by ensuring that the harvest of forests for timber and non-timber products maintains a forest's biodiversity, productivity, and ecological processes, and by respecting the rights of and providing incentives to indigenous people to sustain forest resources. In addition to prohibiting the destruction of natural forests, the FSC safeguards endangered species, and bans toxic pesticides and the planting of genetically modified trees. FSC certified products include lumber, paper, printing, packaging, furniture, and other products made from wood.

LEED—The U.S. Green Building Council provides LEED (Leadership in Energy and Environmental Design) certification for buildings or communities designed and built with environmentally sensitive siting, energy savings, water efficiency, C02 emissions reduction, sustainable materials, improved indoor environmental quality, innovative technology and strategies, and stewardship of resources. It looks at the building life-cycle from design and construction to operations and maintenance, and substantial retrofits. LEED certification applies to commercial real estate, residential homes, schools and hospitals, and even the design or retrofit of neighborhoods.

Rainforest Alliance Certification—The Rainforest Alliance works to conserve biodiversity and ensure sustainable livelihoods by transforming land-use practices, business practices and consumer behavior. It offers certification to farms that protect natural ecosystems and endangered species, do not pollute water bodies, prohibit hunting of wild animals except when done by indigenous groups in a controlled manner, ban the use of certain chemicals and genetically modified crops, and protect workers' rights. As one of the founders of the FSC, it certifies forests and forest products. It also certifies hotels, restaurants and other tourism businesses that meet its environmental, social and economic criteria including the use of clean technologies, waste management and recycling, carbon offsets, biodiversity conservation, cultural preservation, gender equality, and green marketing. The Rainforest Alliance also certifies forestry projects that demonstrate an ability to sequester carbon dioxide and reduce greenhouse gas emissions.

Certified Wildlife Friendly—The Wildlife Friendly Enterprise Network promotes wildlife conservation through certifying products that are linked to conservation actions, and that benefit and involve local individuals and communities living with wildlife. Certified products include alpaca garments, essential oils, chili products, rice, eco-fashion, a community market organization, and a conservation program that helps control bushmeat poaching. Each certified entity is tied to conservation efforts for particular species.

Organizations to Contact

The editors have compiled the following list of organizations concerned with the issues debated in this book. The descriptions are derived from materials provided by the organizations. All have publications or information available for interested readers. The list was compiled on the date of publication of the present volume; the information provided here may change. Be aware that many organizations take several weeks or longer to respond to inquiries, so allow as much time as possible.

Biodiversity Project
4507 N. Ravenswood Ave., No. 106, Chicago, IL   60640
(773) 754-8900
e-mail: project@biodiverse.org
website: www.biodiversityproject.org

Biodiversity Project is a nonprofit organization based in Chicago that helps other nonprofit organizations and coalitions with communications campaigns to protect North America's land and water resources. Its mission is to make people aware of the importance of biodiversity and, through public education and communications programs, empower them to take actions to protect nature. The group's website contains information about the organization's current and past projects, as well as links to a quarterly newsletter and news articles.

Biodiversity Support Program (BSP)
c/o World Wildlife Fund, 1250 24th St. NW, PO Box 97180
Washington, DC   20090-7180
(202) 293-4800
website: www.worldwildlife.org/bsp

The Biodiversity Support Program (BSP), a project of the World Wildlife Fund, The Nature Conservancy, and World Resources Institute, promotes conservation of the world's biological diversity by integrating conservation with social and

economic development, research and analysis, and information exchange and outreach. BSP has conducted conservation
projects in many countries and regions, including ones in
Asia, Africa, Eastern Europe, and Latin America. Its website
provides a link to a list of publications on biodiversity topics
relating to these various projects.

Center for Biodiversity and Conservation, American Museum of Natural History

Central Park West and 79th St., New York, NY   10024
(212) 769-5742 • fax: (212) 769-5292
e-mail: biodiversity@amnh.org
website: http://cbc.amnh.org

The Center for Biodiversity and Conservation was created by
the American Museum of Natural History to advance scientific research in various ecosystems and to use science, education, and outreach to encourage people to participate in the
conservation of biodiversity. The Center publishes a periodic
newsletter, *Lessons in Conservation,* as well as papers, educational materials, field reports, and brochures on conservation
issues. Publications include *Protecting Nature in Your Community* and *Nature in Fragments: The Legacy of Sprawl.*

Conservation International (CI)

2011 Crystal Dr., Suite 500, Arlington, VA   22202
(703) 341-2400
website: www.conservation.org

Conservation International (CI) works to ensure a healthy
planet by protecting biodiversity. CI uses science, field work,
and public policy to help move communities, societies, and
countries toward a smarter, more sustainable development
path that will reduce the human impact on tropical forests,
grasslands, rivers, wetlands, lakes, and the sea. The CI website
is a good source for news and other publications on biodiversity issues. Examples of CI publications include *Climate for
Life* and *A Perfect Storm for the Amazon Wilderness.*

Ecological Society of America (ESA)
1990 M St. NW, Suite 700, Washington, DC   20036
(202) 833-8773 • fax: (202) 833-8775
e-mail: esahq@esa.org
website: www.esa.org

The Ecological Society of America (ESA) is a nonpartisan, nonprofit organization of scientists founded in 1915 to improve communication among ecologists, raise the public's awareness about ecology, increase the resources available for the conduct of ecological science, and promote the use of ecological science in environmental decisionmaking. ESA publications, available on its website, address the interests of diverse readers, including scientists, students, educators, resource managers, and other users of ecological knowledge.

Food and Agriculture Organization
of the United Nations (FAO): Biodiversity
Viale delle Terme di Caracalla, Rome   00153
    Italy
(+39) 06 57051 • fax: (+39) 06 57053152
e-mail: FAO-HQ@fao.org
website: www.fao.org/biodiversity

The Food and Agriculture Organization of the United Nations (FAO) leads international efforts to improve the nutrition, standard of living, and agricultural productivity of rural populations. It provides information, helps developing countries modernize, and acts as a neutral forum where all nations can meet as equals to negotiate agreements and debate policy. Its website on biodiversity explores the connection between biodiversity and food security issues and is a source of publications on biodiversity. Examples include *Save and Grow: A Policymaker's Guide to Sustainable Intensification* and *Biodiversity for Food and Agriculture.*

International Union for the Conservation of Nature and Natural Resources (IUCN)
Rue Mauverney 28, Gland   1196
  Switzerland
+41 (22) 999-0000 • fax: +41 (22) 999-0002
website: www.iucn.org

The International Union for the Conservation of Nature and Natural Resources (IUCN), also often called the World Conservation Union, is a global conservation network of countries, government agencies, nongovernmental organizations (NGOs), scientists, and other experts. The IUCN seeks to encourage the conservation of nature and to ensure that natural resources are used equitably and in ecologically sustainable ways. IUCN publishes *World Conservation Magazine*, and its website contains a wealth of information about biodiversity, including thousands of authoritative publications, reports, guidelines, and databases for conservation and sustainable development. Publications include *Island Invasives, Eradication and Management: Proceedings of the International Conference on Island Invasives* and *Exploring Ecosystem Valuation to Move Towards Net Positive Impact on Biodiversity in the Mining Sector.*

IUCN Global Species Programme Red List Unit
IUCN UK Office, 219c Huntingdon Rd.
Cambridge   CB3 0DL
  United Kingdom
+44 (0) 1223 277966 • fax: +44 (0) 1223 277845
e-mail: redlist@iucn.org
website: www.iucnredlist.org

A project of the International Union for Conservation of Nature and Natural Resources (IUCN), the IUCN Global Species Programme Red List Unit publishes the *IUCN Red List of Threatened Species*, a comprehensive, objective evaluation of the conservation status and risk for extinction of Earth's plant and animal species. The *Red List* is published each year to highlight species that are in danger of extinction. The Red List

Unit website, in addition to providing the current list of threatened species, is a good source for news articles about biodiversity and photos of threatened species.

National Audubon Society (NAS)
225 Varick St., New York, NY 10014
(212) 979-3000
e-mail: education@audubon.org
website: www.audubon.org

The National Audubon Society (NAS) works to conserve and restore natural ecosystems, focusing on birds, other wildlife, and their habitats for the benefit of humans and Earth's biological diversity. It maintains a national network of community-based nature centers and chapters and conducts scientific, educational, and advocacy programs. NAS publishes the bimonthly *Audubon* magazine, and its website contains information on a range of issues related to biodiversity, plus a blog and numerous wildlife videos.

National Council for Science and the Environment (NCSE)
1101 17th St. NW, Suite 250, Washington, DC 20036
(202) 530-5810 • fax: (202) 628-4311
e-mail: NCSE@NCSEonline.org
website: http://ncseonline.org

The National Council for Science and the Environment (NCSE) is a nonprofit organization dedicated to improving the scientific basis for environmental decisionmaking. NCSE conducts a number of educational programs, including one on biodiversity, and its publications include the newsletter *NCSE Quarterly*, as well as news articles and reports. Reports include *2001 Conference Report: Recommendations for Achieving Sustainable Communities* and *Climate Solutions Consensus: What We Know and What to Do About It*.

The Nature Conservancy
4245 N. Fairfax Dr., Suite 100, Arlington, VA 22203-1606
(703) 841-5300
website: www.nature.org

The Nature Conservancy is a leading conservation organization that works to protect ecologically important lands and waters around the globe, on which all life depends. Its website is a source of news and other publications on biodiversity issues, and the group also publishes the *Nature Conservancy* magazine. Feature articles in the magazine include "Nature Makes a Comeback, 60 Years of Conservation" and "Forever Costa Rica."

Seed Savers Exchange
3094 North Winn Rd., Decorah, Iowa   52101
(563) 382-5990 • fax: (563) 382-5872
e-mail: steph@seedsavers.org
website: www.seedsavers.org

The nonprofit Seed Savers Exchange is dedicated to saving North America's diverse, but endangered, garden heritage for future generations by encouraging the collecting, conserving, and sharing of heirloom seeds and plants. It also educates people about the value of genetic and cultural diversity. The group's website provides information about heirloom plant varieties and an extensive catalog of heirloom seeds, which can be purchased online. The online store also features books for children, study guides for teachers, cookbooks, and gardening books.

United Nations Environment Programme World Conservation Monitoring Centre (UNEP-WCMC)
219 Huntingdon Rd., Cambridge   CB3 0DL
   United Kingdom
+44 (0) 1223 277314 • fax: +44 (0) 1223 277136
e-mail: info@unep-wcmc.org
website: www.unep-wcmc.org

The United Nations Environment Programme World Conservation Monitoring Centre (UNEP-WCMC) is a collaboration between the United Nations Environment Programme, an intergovernmental organization, and WCMC, a UK-based charity. It promotes biodiversity and provides authoritative biodiversity information to decisionmakers. The UNEP-WCMC website contains a number of publications on biodiversity and related topics, including databases, tools, books, and reports. Two reports are: *World Atlas of Biodiversity* and *The World's Protected Areas: Status, Value and Prospects in the 21st Century.*

US Fish and Wildlife Service, Endangered Species Program
4401 N. Fairfax Dr., Room 420, Arlington, VA   22203
website: www.fws.gov/endangered

The Endangered Species Program of the US Fish and Wildlife Service is a federal agency primarily responsible for administering the Endangered Species Act (ESA), a law designed to protect endangered and threatened plant and animal species. The agency partners with private and public landowners, states, and foreign governments to protect endangered and threatened species, help these species recover, and conserve species that may be at risk so that they do not become endangered. The agency produces a bimonthly newsletter, *Endangered Species Bulletin,* and its website contains lists of endangered and threatened species, as well as information about species protection.

World Wildlife Fund (WWF)
1250 24th St. NW, PO Box 97180
Washington, DC   20090-7180
(202) 293-4800
website: www.worldwildlife.org

World Wildlife Fund (WWF) is a leading conservation organization dedicated to conserving nature and reducing the threats to Earth's biodiversity. The organization's goal is, by 2020, to conserve fifteen of the world's most ecologically important regions by working with partners to protect and restore species and their habitats, strengthen local communities' ability to conserve their natural resources, change business markets and government policies to reduce the impact of human development and production on the environment, and encourage the public to support conservation. The WWF newsroom is a source of news, press releases, fact sheets, and scientific reports on a wide range of biodiversity topics. Publications include *WWF and Polar Bear Conservation* and *Illegal Fishing in Arctic Waters: Catch of Today, Gone Tomorrow?*

Bibliography

Books

Joshua Bishop | *The Economics of Ecosystems and Biodiversity in Business and Enterprise*, New York: Routledge, 2012.

Eric Chivian and Aaron Bernstein | *Sustaining Life: How Human Health Depends on Biodiversity*, New York: Oxford University Press, 2008.

Cristina Eisenberg | *The Wolf's Tooth: Keystone Predators, Trophic Cascades, and Biodiversity*, Washington, DC: Island Press, 2011.

Paul R. Epstein et al. | *Changing Planet, Changing Health: How the Climate Crisis Threatens Our Health and What We Can Do About It*, Berkeley: University of California Press, 2011.

Paul Gepts et al. | *Biodiversity in Agriculture: Domestication, Evolution, and Sustainability*, Cambridge, UK: Cambridge University Press, 2012.

Gene S. Helfman | *Fish Conservation: A Guide to Understanding and Restoring Global Aquatic Biodiversity and Fishery Resources*, Washington, DC: Island Press, 2007.

Jeffrey S. Levinton | *Marine Biology: Function, Biodiversity, Ecology*, New York: Oxford University Press, 2008.

Anne E. Magurran and Brian J. McGill	*Biological Diversity: Frontiers in Measurement and Assessment,* New York: Oxford University Press, 2011.
Shahid Naeem et al.	*Biodiversity, Ecosystem Functioning, and Human Wellbeing: An Ecological and Economic Perspective,* New York: Oxford University Press, 2009.
Kevin J. O'Brien	*An Ethics of Biodiversity: Christianity, Ecology, and the Variety of Life,* Washington, DC: Georgetown University Press, 2010.
Richard Pearson and American Museum of Natural History	*Driven to Extinction: The Impact of Climate Change on Biodiversity,* New York: Sterling, 2011.
Greg Pyers	*Biodiversity of Rain Forests,* Salt Lake City, UT: Benchmark Books, 2010.
Peter Sale	*Our Dying Planet: An Ecologist's View of the Crisis We Face,* Berkeley: University of California Press, 2011.
John A. Talent	*Earth and Life: Global Biodiversity, Extinction Intervals and Biogeographic Perturbations Through Time,* New York: Springer, 2012.
Mitch Tobin	*Endangered: Biodiversity on the Brink,* Minneapolis, MN: Fulcrum Press, 2010.
United Nations	*The Economics of Ecosystems and Biodiversity in National and International Policy Making (TEEB),* New York: United Nations, 2011.

Periodicals and Internet Sources

Paul Alois and Victoria Cheng	"Keystone Species Extinction Overview," *World's Biggest Problems*, July 2007. www.arlingtoninstitute.org.
Anthony D. Barnosky et al.	"Has the Earth's Sixth Mass Extinction Already Arrived?" *Nature*, March 2, 2011. www.nature.com.
Richard Black	"Businesses 'Profit from Investing in Nature,'" BBC News, July 12, 2010. www.bbc.co.uk.
The Economist	"Beastly Tales: The Latest Estimates on Endangered Species," June 16, 2011. www.economist.com.
Environment News Service	"Biodiversity Losses Accelerate as Ecosystems Approach Tipping Points," May 11, 2010. www.ens -newswire.com.
Christopher D.G. Harley	"Climate Change, Keystone Predation, and Biodiversity Loss," *Science*, November 25, 2011. www.sciencemag.org.
Fangliang He and Stephen P. Hubbell	"Species-Area Relationships Always Overestimate Extinction Rates from Habitat Loss," *Nature*, May 19, 2011. www.nature.com.
Erica R. Hendry	"Five Species Likely to Become Extinct in the Next 40 Years," *Smithsonian Magazine*, August 2010. www.smithsonianmag.com.

The Huffington Post	"Endangered Species Which Need Our Help in 2012," December 30, 2011. www.huffingtonpost.com.
Amina Khan	"Global Species Extinction Isn't Quite So Dire, Study Finds," *Los Angeles Times*, May 21, 2011. http://articles.latimes.com.
Anna Lappé	"The Battle for Biodiversity: Monsanto and Farmers Clash," *The Atlantic*, March 28, 2011. www.theatlantic.com.
Nature Climate Change	"Biodiversity on the Brink," August 26, 2011. www.nature.com.
The New York Times	"How Healthy Are Our Fisheries?" April 20, 2011. www.nytimes.com.
Northwestern University	"Biodiversity: Limit One, Save Many," January 31, 2011. www.northwestern.edu.
Mike Orcutt	"What's the Catch? Researchers Wrangle Over How to Measure Commercial Fishing's Impact on Ocean Biodiversity," *Scientific American*, December 21, 2010. www.scientificamerican.com.
Martin Patience	"China Wakes Up to Biodiversity Threat," BBC News, October 15, 2010. www.bbc.co.uk.
Peter Rothberg	"Barbie's Rainforest Destruction Habit Revealed," *The Nation*, June 13, 2011. www.thenation.com.

Rudy Ruitenberg   "Climate Change Models May Underestimate Extinction, Study Shows," *Businessweek*, January 4, 2012. www.businessweek.com.

Quirin Schiermeier   "Biodiversity's Ills Not All Down to Climate Change," *Nature*, March 21, 2011. www.nature.com.

Science*Daily*   "Marine Biodiversity Loss Due to Global Warming and Predation, Study Predicts," November 28, 2011. www.sciencedaily.com.

Science*Daily*   "New Method for Measuring Biodiversity Makes It Easier to Identify Key Species," February 18, 2008. www.sciencedaily.com.

Science*Daily*   "Ongoing Global Biodiversity Loss Unstoppable with Protected Areas Alone," July 28, 2011. www.science daily.com.

Graham Smith   "Coral Species May Be Extinct Within 50 Years, Warn Scientists as They Reveal Most Endangered," *Daily Mail*, January 11, 2011. www.daily mail.co.uk.

Pete Spotts   "How Long Does It Take Species to Go Extinct? Longer Than Previously Thought," *Christian Science Monitor*, May 18, 2011. www.csmonitor.com.

Jennifer Viegas   "Big Question for 2012: What
                   Animals Could Go Extinct?"
                   Discovery News, December 15, 2011.
                   http://news.discovery.com.

Index

A

Africa, 55, 86, 121
African elephant, 81–82, 86
Agresti, James D., 61–63
Agricultural biodiversity (agro-biodiversity)
  government intervention needed for, 97–98
  high-yield crops deplete, 95–98
  loss of, 95–97
  organic crops and, 177
Agricultural fertilizers, 28–29, 45, 50
Agricultural productivity
  biodiversity loss from, 138–142
  embedded nature of, 141
  future direction of, 142
  new approach to, 139–140
  overview, 138–139
  sustainability of, 140–141
Agriculture and Human Values (magazine), 139
Agroecology, 124, 140–142, 144–145
Air pollution, 21–22, 67
Algae-dominated (eutrophic) state, 28
Alien invasive species, 25–27, 159
Alliance for Zero Extinction, 174
Amazon forest, 28, 66, 116–117, 165, 167
American Bird Conservancy, 174
American Museum of Natural History, 62

Ammonia emissions, 115
Amphibians
  chytrid fungus and, 56
  extinction risks, 24, 37, 74, 92
  GE crops and, 135
  habitats for, 79
An Inconvenient Truth (Gore), 61–63
Animal agriculture
  environmental threat of, 114–119
  factory farming, 112–114
  on farms, 105–106, 114–119
  mitigation of, 119
Antarctic, 40
Antibiotic pollution, 102, 115–116
Aquaculture, 100–102, 127
Arctic sea ice, 40–41
Argentina, 135, 144
Asia, 49, 55, 86, 102
Asner, Greg, 53–54
Atlantic salmon, 100–101
Australia, 84, 86, 93, 135, 166

B

Bacillus thuringiensis bacteria, 124, 131–135
Bald eagles, 77, 149
Bark beetles, 166
Barnosky, Anthony, 69, 70
Bayer company, 125
BBC (news source), 46–47
Bears
  grizzly bears, 76–77, 82, 100, 149
  polar bears, 37, 41, 85